About *The Way Into...*

T0284694

The Way Into... is a major series that provides an accessible and highly usable "guided tour" of the Jewish faith and people, its history and beliefs—in total, a basic introduction to Judaism for adults that will enable them to understand and interact with sacred texts.

The Authors

Each book in the series is written by a leading contemporary teacher and thinker. While each of the authors brings his or her own individual style of teaching to the series, every volume's approach is the same: to help you to learn, in a life-affecting way, about important concepts in Judaism.

The Concepts

Each volume in *The Way Into...* Series explores one important concept in Judaism, including its history, its basic vocabulary, and what it means to Judaism and to us. In the Jewish tradition of study, the reader is helped to interact directly with sacred texts.

The topics to be covered in *The Way Into...* Series:

Torah
Jewish Prayer
Encountering God in Judaism
Jewish Mystical Tradition
Covenant and Commandment
Holiness and Chosenness (Kedushah)
Time
The Natural World
Zion
Tikkun Olam (Repairing the World)
Money and Ownership
Women and Men
Jews and Non-Jews
Varieties of Jewishness

Jewish Lights Books by Lawrence Kushner

The Book of Letters: A Mystical Hebrew Alphabet

The Book of Words: Talking Spiritual Life, Living Spiritual Talk

Eyes Remade for Wonder: A Lawrence Kushner Reader

Filling Words with Light:
Hasidic and Mystical Reflections on Jewish Prayer
with Nehemia Polen

God Was in This Place & I, i Did Not Know:
Finding Self, Spirituality and Ultimate Meaning

Honey from the Rock: An Introduction to Jewish Mysticism

Invisible Lines of Connection: Sacred Stories of the Ordinary

Jewish Spirituality: A Brief Introduction for Christians

The River of Light: Jewish Mystical Awareness

The Way Into Jewish Mystical Tradition

For Children

Because Nothing Looks Like God
with Karen Kushner

The Book of Miracles: A Young Person's Guide
to Jewish Spiritual Awareness

How Does God Make Things Happen?
with Karen Kushner
(SkyLight Paths Publishing)

In God's Hands
with Gary Schmidt

What Does God Look Like?
with Karen Kushner
(SkyLight Paths Publishing)

Where Is God?
with Karen Kushner
(SkyLight Paths Publishing)

Fiction

Kabbalah: A Love Story
(Morgan Road Books, Fall 2006)

The Way Into

Jewish Mystical Tradition

Lawrence Kushner

דרך למוד דרך למוד דרך למוד
דרך למוד

JEWISH LIGHTS Publishing

Woodstock, Vermont

The Way Into Jewish Mystical Tradition

2006 Second Printing, Quality Paperback Edition
2004 First Printing, Quality Paperback Edition
© 2001 by Lawrence Kushner

All rights reserved. No part of this book may be reproduced or transmitted in any form or by any means, electronic or mechanical, including photocopying, recording, or by any information storage and retrieval system, without permission in writing from the publisher.

For information regarding permission to reprint material from this book, please mail or fax your request in writing to Jewish Lights Publishing, Permissions Department, at the address / fax number listed below, or e-mail your request to permissions@jewishlights.com.

Library of Congress Cataloging-in-Publication Data

Kushner, Lawrence, 1943–
The way into Jewish mystical tradition / by Lawrence Kushner.
p. cm.
Includes bibliographical references (p.) and index.
ISBN 1-58023-029-6 (hbk)
1. Mysticism-Judaism. 2. Spiritual life-Judaism. 3. Cabala-History. I. Title.
BM723 .K89 2001
296.7'12-dc21

00-012716

10   9   8   7   6   5   4   3   2

Manufactured in the United States of America
Jacket design by Glenn Suokko
Text design by Glenn Suokko

Published by Jewish Lights Publishing
A Division of LongHill Partners, Inc.
Sunset Farm Offices, Route 4, P.O. Box 237
Woodstock, VT 05091
Tel: (802) 457-4000   Fax: (802) 457-4004
www.jewishlights.com

The publisher gratefully acknowledges the contribution of Rabbi Sheldon Zimmerman to the creation of this series. In his lifelong work of bringing a greater appreciation of Judaism to all people, he saw the need for *The Way Into...* and inspired us to act on it.

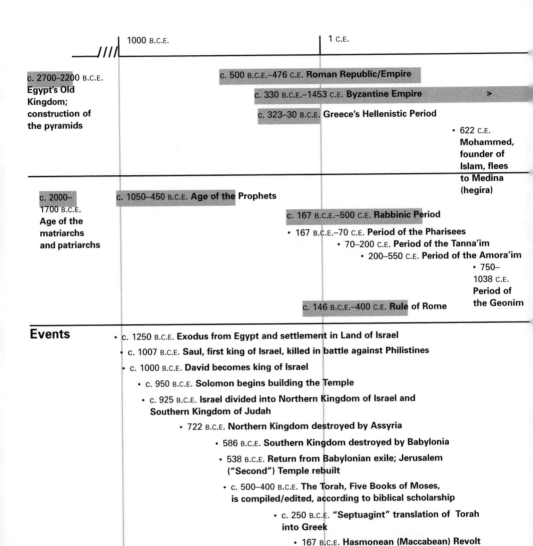

1000 B.C.E.   1 C.E.

c. 2700–2200 B.C.E.
**Egypt's Old
Kingdom;
construction of
the pyramids**

c. 500 B.C.E.–476 C.E. **Roman Republic/Empire**

c. 330 B.C.E.–1453 C.E. **Byzantine Empire** >

c. 323–30 B.C.E. **Greece's Hellenistic Period**

• 622 C.E.
**Mohammed,
founder of
Islam, flees
to Medina
(hegira)**

c. 2000–
1700 B.C.E.
**Age of the
matriarchs
and patriarchs**

c. 1050–450 B.C.E. **Age of the Prophets**

c. 167 B.C.E.–500 C.E. **Rabbinic Period**

• 167 B.C.E.–70 C.E. **Period of the Pharisees**
• 70–200 C.E. **Period of the Tanna'im**
• 200–550 C.E. **Period of the Amora'im**

• 750–
1038 C.E.
**Period of
the Geonim**

c. 146 B.C.E.–400 C.E. **Rule of Rome**

Events

• c. 1250 B.C.E. **Exodus from Egypt and settlement in Land of Israel**
• c. 1007 B.C.E. **Saul, first king of Israel, killed in battle against Philistines**
• c. 1000 B.C.E. **David becomes king of Israel**
  • c. 950 B.C.E. **Solomon begins building the Temple**
  • c. 925 B.C.E. **Israel divided into Northern Kingdom of Israel and
    Southern Kingdom of Judah**
    • 722 B.C.E. **Northern Kingdom destroyed by Assyria**
      • 586 B.C.E. **Southern Kingdom destroyed by Babylonia**
      • 538 B.C.E. **Return from Babylonian exile; Jerusalem
        ("Second") Temple rebuilt**
      • c. 500–400 B.C.E. **The Torah, Five Books of Moses,
        is compiled/edited, according to biblical scholarship**
        • c. 250 B.C.E. **"Septuagint" translation of Torah
          into Greek**
          • 167 B.C.E. **Hasmonean (Maccabean) Revolt**
            • 70 C.E. **Rome destroys Second Temple**
              • c. 200 **The Mishnah compiled/
                edited by Rabbi Judah ha-Nasi**
                • c. 300–600 **The Babylonian
                  and Palestinian Talmuds are
                  compiled/edited**

1000 C.E.   2000 C.E.

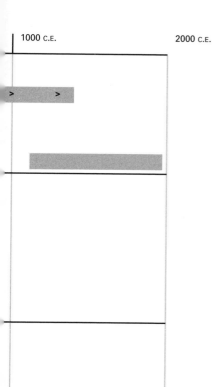

- c. 1040–1105 **Rashi, French Bible and Talmud scholar and creator of line-by-line commentary on the Torah**
    - 1178 **Maimonides (1135–1204) completes his code of Jewish law, the *Mishneh Torah***
        - c. 1295 ***The Zohar,* Kabbalistic work of mystical teaching, composed**
            - 1492 **Jews expelled from Spain**
                - 1565 **Joseph Caro publishes *Shulchan Arukh,* the standard code of Jewish law and practice**
                    - 1654 **First Jewish settlement in North America at New Amsterdam**
                        - 1700–1760 **Israel Baal Shem Tov, founder of Hasidism**
                            - 1729–1786 **Moses Mendelssohn, "Father of the Jewish Enlightenment"**
                                - 1801–1888 **Samson Raphael Hirsch, founder of "modern Orthodoxy"**
                                    - 1836 **Yeshiva University founded**
                                        - 1873; 1875 **Reform Judaism in U.S. establishes
                                          Union of American Hebrew Congregations and Hebrew Union College**
                                            - 1887 **Conservative Judaism's Jewish Theological Seminary founded**
                                                - 1897 **Theodor Herzl convenes first Zionist Congress**
                                                    - 1933–1945 **The Holocaust (Shoah)**
                                                        - 1935 **Mordecai Kaplan establishes the Jewish Reconstructionist Foundation**
                                                            - 1948 **Birth of the State of Israel**

for Jim Ball & Anita Diamant,
family

Contents

Part Two

Part Three

Acknowledgments

I want to acknowledge some of my friends and mentors who have patiently helped me discover and decode many of the following mystical texts. Lawrence Fine, Arthur Green, Moshe Waldoks, Daniel Matt (who first introduced me to the mysteries of the *Zohar*), Zalman Schachter-Shalomi (who showed us all the way), and especially Ed Feld and Nehemia Polen have all been my teachers. Their erudition and generosity have been invaluable; any errors, however, are entirely my own.

The present volume grew out of an introductory seminar for rabbinic students that Dean Aaron Panken originally invited me to teach at the Hebrew Union College–Jewish Institute of Religion in New York a few years ago. I am grateful for his vision and confidence and for the questions and enthusiasm of my students.

I also want to express my gratitude to Sandra Korinchak, editor of this series, who has, with unflappable aplomb, kept me on time and honest; Seymour Rossel, the editor of this book, whose gift with words, irrepressible good humor, and encyclopedic knowledge of Judaism have, time and again, turned musings into good writing; and especially Stuart Matlins, publisher of Jewish Lights Publishing, for having the trust in my competence to undertake such a project and for giving me such a wonderful challenge. Finally, Karen, bride of my youth, again and again you bring life to my life.

Introduction

Psalm 19

Our guided tour of the Jewish mystical imagination begins with
Psalm 19. The biblical poet elegantly sets before us the primary
themes and the sequence of their occurrence in the formation of a
personal, Jewish mystical world-view.

More than twenty-five years ago, Professor Michael Fishbane
of the University of Chicago showed me how the poem easily divides
itself into three natural parts. The psalmist begins with an experience
of creation that transcends language. Such reverence seems beyond
the power of words. In the second part, the psalm shifts, abruptly, to
a paean to God's Torah and its inherent value for those who follow
its instruction. Revelation both enlightens and rewards us. The
psalmist concludes with a confession of anxiety over the commission
of deliberate and inadvertent sins. Ultimately, the unknown biblical
poet yearns only for personal redemption and the worthiness necessary to stand in God's presence. Here is the psalm:

> For the leader, a Psalm of David:
> The heavens rehearse the presence of God, just as the
> firmament proclaims God's doing. Day after day speaking
> gushes forth, just as night after night wisdom is whispered.
> But of course there can be no speaking, nor can there be
> any words; indeed, the voices of the heavens and the fir-
> mament cannot even be heard. Still their voice reverberates
> throughout creation, their words to the ends of the earth.

With them, God has made a tent for the sun. It is like a bride-groom emerging from his marriage canopy, like an athlete in prime, ready for the contest. He comes out at one end of the heavens and his course leads him to the other. No one can hide from the heat of the sun.

The Torah of God is really very simple, reviving the soul; the testimony of God is sure, giving wisdom to the fool. The statutes of God are right, rejoicing the heart; the command-ment of God is clear, enlightening the eyes. The reverence of God is pure, enduring forever; the judgments of God are true and righteous altogether. More precious than gold, even than all the finest gold; it is sweeter than honey drip-ping from the comb. For this reason, your servant is eager to follow them; the reward is great.

Who could possibly be aware of every mistake? O let me be free from inadvertent wrongdoing. And keep your servant far from deliberate sins; let arrogance have no power over me. Only then will I be innocent and clear of great transgression. May these words of my mouth and the meditation of my heart be acceptable before You, O God, my rock, and my redeemer.

In this simple, tripartite form we have a concise summary of the mystic way of Judaism: (1) an inexpressible reverence before the awe and mystery of creation, (2) the conviction that sacred text contains the key to unlocking the secret of being, and (3) a resul-tant yearning to lead a life of holiness and righteousness.

We shall examine these primary themes of the Jewish mystical tradition through close readings of classical and some less well-known texts. For each text, we will carefully unpack the key ideas and demonstrate how they might be part of a contemporary, per-sonal, mystical Jewish world-view.

The Jewish Mystical Tradition

Jewish mysticism (and Kabbalah, which is one of its best-known manifestations) is an attitude toward reality, a way of understanding, organizing, and enriching Jewish religious life. For this reason, Jewish mysticism is not something one can "do" outside normative religious practice. Like all varieties of mysticism, it is predicated on the possibility of unmediated and personal communion with God. The mystic does not merely want to do what God wants; the mystic wants to see what God sees, to know what God knows! The mystic is therefore even more than God's partner or agent; the mystic is a *manifestation* of the Holy One of all Being. Through awareness, the instruction of sacred tradition, and finally right action, the mystic believes that he or she is capable of restoring harmony both to this world and to worlds on high.

Historians often divide the Jewish mystical tradition into eras: biblical (Moses, Elijah, Isaiah, Ezekiel; Israel, 1300–400 B.C.E.); *Heikhalot,* or celestial palaces, and *yordei merkavah,* seekers of Ezekiel's chariot (beginning circa first century B.C.E.); *Hasidei Ashkenaz* (Germany, tenth to twelfth centuries); pre-Zoharic Spain (Provence, end of the twelfth century); Spanish Kabbalah (Catalonia and Castile, end of the thirteenth century; theosophy of the *sefirot*), the meditative or ecstatic Kabbalah of men like Abraham Abulafia; Lurianic Kabbalah (sixteenth-century Safed); and finally Hasidism (eighteenth-century Poland).

Naturally, each of these flowerings developed unique ideas. Some enriched and shaped the imagination of subsequent generations of mystics, and others did not. The *Heikhalot* mystics, for example, were fascinated with an intricate metaphor called *shiur koma,* which attempted to describe the size of God's body (!), and the followers of Luria were fascinated with the possibility of the transmigration of souls and past lives. Such ideas, while exciting and important in their own time, failed to attain prominence in successive eras of the Jewish mystical imagination. The present volume is not a systematic intellectual history. Our goal in the following pages is to focus instead on ideas that, once they appeared, remained central to all future expressions of mysticism and that remain fecund to this day. Ezekiel's vision of the chariot, the sefirotic diagram of divine emanation, and Isaac Luria's notion of God's self-contraction, for example, continue to play a vibrant and formative role even in the work of contemporary mystics.

In the same vein, I have omitted discussion of what is called "Practical Kabbalah." Practical Kabbalah claims to be able to take advantage of the mystic's intimacy with God and to use that knowledge to manipulate the universe in magical ways. (This may also explain the confusion in the popular mind with mysticism and such quasi-mystical categories as magic, superstition, golems, dybbuks, and reincarnation.) Mystics may claim unique insight into the ultimate nature of reality, but that does not make them sorcerers or wizards.

What Makes This Book Different

Our guided tour will be organized around fifty Jewish mystical ideas. Each one is presented in a biblical verse, classical maxim, or phrase. To help preserve their traditional flavor (and entice the beginning student), each is also offered in its original Hebrew or Aramaic and then in transliteration. Each idea, in turn, is illustrated with one or more classical texts.

The translations are my own, with the exceptions of those on pages 26–27, 57, 86, 110–111, 118, 121, and 150–151. I have not translated the titles of most of the Hebrew and Aramaic sources for two reasons. First, because they are so poetic and allusive, they defy literal translation. Second, with only rare exceptions, no one knows them by any other name. (No one, for example, calls the *Zohar* "The Book of Radiance," even though that is what it means in English.) Whenever possible, I have tried to choose texts representing the broadest possible range of the tradition.

My primary goal, however, has been to offer the reader sources that, when taken together, might describe the outlines of what I believe is a maturing, contemporary Jewish mysticism. My assumption throughout is that the reader is interested not only in *learning about* the Jewish mystical tradition but also in *trying it on* for size. Rather than attempt a comprehensive anthology, therefore, we shall examine only those elements of the tradition that remain vital to this day. Indeed, I am convinced that Jewish mysticism continues to provide a coherent and compelling way of making sense of contemporary religious reality. Like Jewish mystics of all generations, we too stand dumbfounded before the mystery of how the One could become many and how the many might again become One.

Our triptych of Jewish mystical tradition begins in Part One with the theme of the first third of Psalm 19, our wonder and amazement at creation, the unfathomable mystery of being, the PRESENCE of God. This will lead us to an examination of the mystic NOTHINGNESS and then to the ineffable NAME of God itself.

Part Two, drawing on the theme developed in the middle of the psalm, will focus on the Jewish mystic's return to the documents of revelation. Here we shall consider the TRUTH of sacred text and how, through it, we might comprehend the ORGANISM of being, until we understand that our own CONSCIOUSNESS is itself a dimension of being.

Finally, in Part Three, we shall turn our attention to the concluding imagery of the psalm. Here the biblical poet, having attained heightened awareness, now seeks to become a better PERSON. In Jewish mysticism this can only be effectuated through right acting, through DEED. Ultimately, the mystic path leaves us with a YEARNING to share the light with everyone and transform ordinary, mundane reality into holiness.

Part One

The heavens rehearse the presence of God.
—PSALM 19:2

1

Presence

It's not that God can be found everywhere, but that everywhere (and everyone) is a manifestation of the Divine. Everything exists within God. In moments of heightened awareness, human beings realize their continuous dependence on and presence within God. The Hebrew *kavod*, customarily translated as "glory," might be more appropriately rendered "presence." Let us begin now with the first part of Psalm 19, the presence of God.

1. God's presence is the fullness of all the world. —Isaiah 6:3

מלא כל הארץ כבודו
Melo khol ha-aretz kevodo

Legacy of Wonder

Abraham Joshua Heschel, *God in Search of Man*[1]

Abraham Joshua Heschel is easily the best-known mystical teacher of the last generation. Born in Warsaw in 1907, scion of a Hasidic dynasty, Heschel was uniquely qualified to combine Western scholarship with Eastern mysticism. Heschel's mysticism—like most Jewish mysticism—was one of political activism. An outspoken critic of American involvement in Vietnam, he was literally on the front lines of the Civil Rights Movement as well. The

Encyclopedia Judaica, in its entry on "Negro-Jewish Relations," includes a photograph of the march from Selma to Montgomery, Alabama. These were frightening times; protesters had been (and would yet be) murdered. Leading the march were Roy Wilkins, Ralph Abernathy, Martin Luther King, Jr., and Abraham Heschel. Heschel died in 1972; he was perhaps the last rebbe educated as a boy in the living community of Polish Hasidim.

The following passage is taken from Heschel's classic *God in Search of Man: A Philosophy of Judaism*. In his distinctive poetic and aphoristic style, Heschel expresses the primary tenet of the Jewish mystical imagination: The whole world is filled with the presence of God. Or, in the words of Isaiah 6:3, "God's presence is the fullness of the world." There is no place without the Divine. In Heschel's formulation, wonderment is the touchstone for all spiritual life. The beginning of religious awareness is standing astonished, reverent, and chastened before the mystery of being. Heschel cautions us that taking things for granted invariably seals us off, not only from novelty and surprise but also from life itself. For Heschel, our chronic dullness to wonderment is the beginning of sinfulness. There is simply more to reality than meets the eye. The closer we look, the more we discover hidden layers of being, and this invariably leads us to God.

> Among the many things that religious tradition holds in store for us is a *legacy of wonder*. The surest way to suppress our ability to understand the meaning of God and the importance of worship is *to take things for granted*. Indifference to the sublime wonder of living is the root of sin. (43)
>
> [Citing Nachmanides, *Commentary* on Exodus 13:16] The belief in "the hidden miracles is the basis for the entire Torah. A man has no share in the Torah, unless he believes that all things and all events in the life of the individual as well as in the life of society are miracles. There is no such thing as the natural course of events...." (51)

The beginning of awe is wonder, and the beginning of wisdom is awe.... Awe is a way of being in rapport with the mystery of all reality. The awe that we sense or ought to sense when standing in the presence of a human being is a moment of intuition for the likeness of God which is concealed in his essence. Not only man; even inanimate things stand in a relation to the Creator. The secret of every being is the divine care and concern that are invested in it. Something sacred is at stake in every event. (74)

2. The power of the Creator within each created thing

כח הפועל בנפעל
Koach ha-Poel benifal

Power of the Creator

Menachem Nachum Twersky of Chernobyl, *Me'or Eina'im* [2]

According to classical Hasidism, the power of the Creator resides within each created thing. Hasidism is the most recent flowering of the Jewish mystical impulse. Beginning in mid-eighteenth-century Poland as an ecstatic folk revival, Hasidism understood communion with God as the primary goal of religious life and made it available to the masses. The movement was founded by Israel ben Eliezer (1700–1760), who came to be known as the Baal Shem Tov, or, after the initials of his Hebrew name, the BeSHT. He preached a Judaism that even the unlearned could easily embrace. Each Hasid became the disciple of a particular rabbi, or rebbe, who served as spiritual mentor. The BeSHT had four primary students, each of whom in turn generated his own circle of disciples: Dov Baer, the Maggid of Mezritch; Pinchas Shapiro of Koretz; Yaakov Yosef of Polnoye; and the author of the following passage, Menachem Nachum Twersky of Chernobyl (1730–1797). Nachum worked as a teacher and lived in poverty.

Like the majority of the literature of theoretical Hasidism (as opposed to its legends and stories), this passage is woven into a teaching on the weekly Torah portion. A canvas painted by Claude Monet has value and power even if the painting itself is of apparently inferior artistic quality. The mere fact that the great impressionist master painted it makes it instructive and therefore significant. The power of the creator, in other words, remains within the creation. In the same way, all of creation, "the fullness of the world," is likewise a manifestation of—and therefore a mechanism for returning to—the Creator. We can access the Creator everywhere.

> God is the fullness of the world; there is no place empty of the divine. There is nothing besides God and everything that exists comes from God. And, for this reason, the power of the Creator resides within each created thing. (14)

3.   There is no place without God's presence
לית אתר פנוי מניה
Leit atar panui minei

The Sand beneath My Feet
Kalonymus Kalman Shapira of Piesetzna, *Benei Makhshava Tovah*[3]

Following World War II, while clearing land for new construction on the site of what had once been the Warsaw Ghetto, a worker unearthed a container filled with Hebrew manuscripts. They were the writings of Kalonymous Kalman Shapira of Piesetzna (Pee-ah-SETZ-nah, 1889–1943). Kalonymous Kalman was born in Grodzisk, Poland, and died in the Trawniki concentration camp. His biographer, Dr. Nehemia Polen of Boston's Hebrew College, notes that the Piesetzner's book *Eish Kodesh,* "Holy Fire," was the last work of Hasidism written on Polish soil. For Kalonymous Kalman,

God can be found everywhere and within everything—not merely in the first springtime flowers or the majesty of the mountains, but even in apparently ungodly and irrelevant things like grains of sand. Everything dissolves into and is nullified within God. Indeed, the only impediment to such cosmic vision is our refusal to see ourselves as indistinguishable manifestations of the divine unity underlying all creation, the mother lode of all meaning. In such moments of heightened awareness, the mystic realizes that God is not *other* than the world, but that being is itself made *of* God. In the words of one ancient maxim: *Min ha-olam ve-ad ha-olam ata Ayl,* "From one end of being unto the other, You are God."

The following passage is taken from one of the Piesetzner's earlier works, *Benei Makhshava Tovah,* a meditative journal for those seeking to create a spiritual community.

> I may not be able to see it right now, but the Holy One fills all creation, being is made of God, you and I, everything is made of God—even the grains of sand beneath my feet, the whole world is included and therefore utterly nullified within God—while I, in my stubborn insistence on my own autonomy and independence, only succeed in banishing myself from any possibility of meaning whatsoever. (33)

The Castle of Illusions
Israel Baal Shem Tov, *Keter Shem Tov*[4]

A similar way of suggesting that God's presence permeates all creation can be found in the following popular story attributed to Israel Baal Shem Tov (whom we shall discuss in section 9). The reason we cannot readily see the divine presence, suggests the teaching, is that the world of our senses is illusory. However, through perseverance and devotion, we can access the ultimate nature of reality. The story appears in *Keter Shem Tov* ("The Crown of a Good Name"), an anthology of the Baal Shem Tov's teachings assembled from the writings of Yaakov Yosef of Polnoye in 1794 (see section 16).

> And some say that the Holy One does this in order to appear to a person that He is distant, and so that the person should strive to get very close. The Baal Shem Tov, his memory is a blessing, used to tell the following parable before the blowing of the *shofar* [on Rosh Hashanah]: "Once there was a very wise king. He made [an] illusory [castle with illusory] walls, towers and gates. Then he commanded that [his subjects] should come to him through the [illusory walls and] gates and the towers. Then he scattered before each and every gate royal treasures. [In this way] when someone came to the first gate, he took the money and left. And so it went [with one seeker after another] until the beloved son came with great determination and proceeded [to walk through one wall after another] right up to his father the king. Then he realized that there was nothing separating himself from his father. Everything was an illusion." (13)

4. The light of the Divine Presence is everywhere

אור השכינה בכל היקום

Or ha-Shekhinah be-khol ha-yekum

Invitation to Awareness

Abraham Isaac Ha-Kohen Kook, *Orot Ha-Kodesh*[5]

Rav Abraham Isaac Ha-Kohen Kook (1865–1935) was the first Ashkenazi chief rabbi of prestate Israel. Trained in Talmud in Lithuania, Kook was a prolific mystical author. His published essays, theology, meditations, and poetry fill dozens of volumes. His

Hebrew is rich but dense. Throughout his writing we find the theme of the omnipresence of the Divine and a corresponding respect for all human beings, whether they be pious Orthodox Jews, secular Zionists, or adherents of other religions. It is difficult to overestimate the importance of his spiritual leadership and example.

The story is told of how Rav Kook dealt with the news that the manager of Jerusalem's only movie theater had decided to keep it open in violation of the Sabbath. Kook literally took to the streets. He stationed himself in silence on the corner in front of the movie house. One by one, as prospective patrons passed their sainted rabbi, they found themselves unable to enter. The battle was won without a shot being fired. The story illustrates an important principle about Kook's teaching and model (which reappears again and again throughout the history of Jewish mysticism). People are assumed to be fundamentally good. They do not need coercion or force to do the right thing; they require only reminding and encouragement.

The following passage is from *Orot Ha-Kodesh* ("The Lights of Holiness"). Next to his short classic on repentance, *Orot Ha-Teshuvah* ("The Lights of Repentance"), *Orot Ha-Kodesh* is Kook's best-known work. It is usually published in four volumes. Here we meet a man filled with optimism and enthusiasm. The divine reality can be found everywhere, realized through our every action.

If you want, O creature of flesh and blood, contemplate the light of God's presence throughout all creation. Contemplate the ecstasy of spiritual existence and how it suffuses every dimension of life—spiritual and material. Right there before the vision of your body and the vision of your soul.

Meditate on the wonders of creation and the divine life within them. Not in some diluted form, as a mere performance distant from your vision but instead, know it as the reality within which you live.

Know yourself and know your world. Know the meditations of your own heart and of every sentient being. Locate the Source of Life deep within you, high above you and all around you—the wondrous splendor of life within which you dwell.

Now raise the love you feel within you to the source of her strength and the ecstasy of her glory. Let her blossom within every meditation. For the cascade of the Soul of the Life of the worlds is a splendor only diminished by the vantage point of the one who seeks to understand.

See the lights and see what is within them. Don't let the holy Names and phrases and letters overwhelm your soul for they have been given over into your hand and not you into theirs.

Go *all* the way up! The strength is yours—wings of spirit like mighty eagles. Don't weaken them, lest they weaken you. But seek them and they will be there for you at once.

So precious and sacred are the manifestations of this reality to us! They are an obligation for us along with all those of more limited spiritual vision. Once we attain a life of awareness, we must not stray from that supernal point. The light always flows from that which cannot be fathomed toward that which can. It emanates from the light of the One without end.

We are each summoned to delight in the ecstasy of heaven, with each individual thought which is all part of the great unity from which all life issues. (83–84)

2

Nothing

God's ubiquity evokes oceanic imagery for mystics of all traditions. As a drop of water dissolved into the sea, so we are waves in an ocean of God. And, like fishes unable to comprehend the ocean within which they live, we too must push our language and imagery to describe the divine All. The most common word Jewish mystics choose to describe God is "Nothing." However, as we shall see, the God they describe is much more than nothing.

5. My help will come from Nothing. —Psalm 121:1
מאין יבא עזרי
Mei-Ayin yavo ezri

Psalm 121:1 is customarily rendered as "I lift up my eyes to the mountains, from where will my help come?" The Hebrew *mei-Ayin*, "from where," can also be read as "*from Nothing* will my help come." This is far from the nihilism it first seems to connote. Indeed, for Jewish mystical tradition, the word *Ayin*, "Nothing," has profound, cosmic significance. Let us begin with its opposite, *yesh*.

Yesh means "somethingness," or better, simply "isness." In modern Hebrew, if you want to say you have something, you say, "*yesh li*," literally, "there is to me." The opposite of *yesh* is *Ayin*.

It means "Nothingness"—not zip or *gornicht* as in Yiddish, but the absence of any "thingness" and, therefore, the absence of definitions or boundaries. If some "thing" were no "thing," then it would be literally boundless. Therefore *Ayin* is also without beginning, without end; *Ayin* is another name for eternity.

Jewish mystical tradition invests these two words with cosmic, metaphysical significance. *Yesh* comes to refer to the created world, the one in which we spend most of our time. *Yesh* connotes temporal, material, even psychological reality. It is a reality of bounded and defined things, each with beginnings and ends and life spans. For every thing that "is" must ultimately come to an end.

Ayin, on the other hand, connotes not the absence of being, but the absence of any boundaries—that is, no "thing," a *nothing* that encompasses all creation. *Ayin* is therefore the font of all being, the substrate of creation. The Kabbalists called God *Ayn Sof*, endless. Not only can't you own it, you cannot alter it, change it, or affect it in any way whatsoever. You cannot point to it. You can't even accurately say as much about it as we've already said. It is as if we were waves and it were the ocean. You and I, this book in your hands, the trees, the people we love, even the love itself, all of creation—they are all the waves, *yesh*, made of that ocean of *Ayin*, manifestations of that great underlying nothingness and oneness of all being.

A Drop in the Ocean

Yechiel Michal of Zlochov, *Yosher Divrei Emet*[1]

The following passage comes from a collection of Hasidic teachings and homilies arranged by Meshullam Feibush of Zabrazh entitled *Yosher Divrei Emet*. It was first published in 1792, making it part of the earliest strata of Hasidic literature. This particular teaching is cited in the name of Yechiel Michal of Zlochov, who in turn attributes it to a sermon he heard delivered on Shavuot 1777 by his teacher, Dov Baer of Mezritch. In it, Dov Baer, or, as he is often known, "The Great *Maggid* [or Storyteller]," uses the notions of *yesh* and *Ayin* in a kind of intellectual sleight of hand, a linguistic shell game, turning their normal usage inside out. He teaches us that understanding the real difference between *yesh* and *Ayin* (something and Nothing) ultimately yields the meaning of life itself. He begins by talking about those who yearn to become one with God through what is called *devekut* (see section 39), to lose themselves in the momentary astonishment that all being is a manifestation of God.

And they yearn to make themselves one with the Holy One, likening themselves to nothingness *(Ayin).* They understand that were it not for the power of the Creator who continuously creates and sustains them each moment, they would be nothing, just as they were before the creation. For indeed, there is nothing in the world except for God.

It is just the opposite of what everyone else in the world thinks. They assume that when they do not merge with their Creator but cleave instead to the things and matters of this world, that they amount to something *(yesh)* in their own eyes. They imagine that they are important. But how could anyone who might not wake up the next morning be important? "One night it's here, the next it's gone!" [Jonah 4:10.] As we read in Psalms [144:4], "their days pass away like a shadow," even while they're alive, it's all a show of vanity.

In this way, if they think they are something *(yesh),* then alas, they are nothing *(ayin).* On the other hand, if, because of their fusion with the Creator, cleaving with all their physical and mental powers, they think of themselves as nothing, then they are very great indeed. They are like the branch of a tree that realizes it is part of one organic unity with its root. And the root, of course, is the One without end—the *Ayn Sof,* the One of Nothing. So, if the branch is one with the root and the root is the One of Nothing, then the branch too ceases to exist as an independent thing; it is nothing.

It's like a single drop of water fallen into the sea. It has returned to its source. It is one with the ocean. Now it's no longer possible to identify it as an independent thing in any way whatsoever. (sec. 14)

The Ocean and the Waves

Richard L. Rubenstein, *Morality and Eros*[2]

This metaphor that God is the Ocean of Being also finds elegant expression in the writing of the contemporary Jewish theologian Richard L. Rubenstein. One of the more controversial teachers of this generation, Rubenstein's restless and penetrating intellect has led him from psychoanalysis to death-of-God theology (his most famous work is *After Auschwitz*) to working with the Reverend Sun Myung Moon. The following passage needs no explanation.

Perhaps the best available metaphor for the conception of God as the Holy Nothingness is that God is the ocean and we are the waves. In some sense each wave has its moment in which it is distinguishable as a somewhat separate entity. Nevertheless, no wave is entirely distinct from the ocean which is its substantial ground. The waves are surface manifestations of the ocean. Our knowledge of the ocean is largely dependent on the way it manifests itself in the waves.

The waves are caught in contradictory tendencies. They are the resultants of forces which allow them their moment of somewhat discrete existence. At the same time, they are wholly within the grasp of greater tendencies which ultimately collapse them into the oceanic ground out of which they have come and from which they have never really separated themselves. So it is with all life. All living organisms seek to maintain their individual existence, yet there is absolutely nothing in them which does not derive from their originating ground. This is especially evident in the most intimate of all human activities, sexual love. Nothing could be more private or personally involving. Nevertheless, at no time is the individual more in the grip of universal forces than in the act of love. Furthermore, only to the extent that the individual is capable of letting these overwhelming forces flow through him of their own accord will the act of love be complete and without flaw. Only he who has the capacity totally to lose himself in love can thereby be fulfilled. (186–187)

6. Every moment God sustains all creation!

בכל רגע משפיע שפע לברואיו ולכל העולמות

Be-khol rega mashpia shefa livruav u-lekhol ha-olamot

Continuous Creation

Levi Yitzchak of Berditchev, *Kedushat Levi*[3]

If God is the Ocean of all Being, then our customary notion of a transcendent creator God who brought the world into being at the beginning of time is no longer adequate. Creation is not an act or an event that happened once and for all in the distant past, but something present also at this very moment. Creation is continuous.

The following passage is the first teaching in Levi Yitzchak of Berditchev's (1740–1810) collected sermons, *Kedushat Levi*. It is a commentary on the opening verse of Genesis. Here we encounter a more sustained exposition of how God's creative presence pervades everything. For Levi Yitzchak, without God's continuous creative power at each and every moment, creation would revert to primordial chaos. To have such an epiphany—to realize that right now, at this very moment, the one who is reading these words is being created by God—is to lose our ordinary sense of self and enter the *Ayin*, or mystical Nothingness of God. Right now, as at every moment, there is only God.

"In the beginning, God created the heaven and the earth..." (Genesis 1:1) All of being—the Creator, God created everything and God *is* everything, perpetually influencing everything without interruption. Every single moment God nourishes creation—all the worlds and all the heavenly temples and all the messengers and all the holy creatures who sustain the divine chariot. [See section 27.]

For this reason we say [in the morning liturgy just following the *Barekhu* or "Call to Worship"]: "Praised are You, God, who creates light and who creates darkness." We do not say, "...Who created light and who created darkness." Instead we only read, "...Who creates..." in the present tense! [This teaches us] that God is creating every moment. Every moment God nourishes every living creature. Everything is from God and God is complete, the One of All Being.

Thus, when a person enters this *Ayin* [this divine Nothingness of all Being] (see section 5), aware now that he is nothing at all, that there is only the Creator who [continuously] gives him strength, then the Name of God, as it were, enters the present tense and God's Name becomes the One who creates, even at this very moment!

Indeed, whenever a person regards himself [as a discrete, independent being], he is no longer within the *Ayin*, but has returned to the level of *Yesh* ["somethingness," everyday reality]. And, in the same way, the Name of the Creator then reverts to [the past tense] "...the One who *created*," a way of thinking that assumes that God has already created everything [and left, or is no longer needed]. That is why we say [in the morning blessings] "...Who created human beings with wisdom." Wisdom [a technical term referring to a dimension of God removed from God's ultimate Nothingness] connotes the level of *Yesh*, somethingness. And for this reason "created" [in the past tense] is used instead of "creates" [in the present].

Similarly this is also spoken of in the writings of Isaac Luria [see section 38]. He teaches that when it says that "God is king," this alludes to *Ayin*, since if God is king it means, in effect, that God is nourishing us [at this very moment]. And this is what we mean by *Ayin*, for [in such a state of awareness] we are absolutely nothing. It is only God, [continuously] bestowing life on us. Indeed, this *Ayin* guides everything that is beyond what is natural, while the *Yesh* in turn governs the natural order. (1:1)

Levi Yitzchak, in a move typical of Jewish mysticism, here shifts from theogony to ethics. He reads, in the imagery of Ezekiel's vision of "creatures dashing to and fro," our own moving from an awareness of the mystical Nothingness of God to the everyday business of trying to be a decent human being in this world of *Yesh*, somethingness.

Furthermore this fusion whereby we join the *Yesh* with the *Ayin* is accomplished through the performance of sacred deeds and Torah, as we read in Ezekiel 1:14, "The holy creatures dashing to and fro..." And this is also what is alluded to in the *Zohar Hadash* III:53b when it says that "sacred deeds and Torah are both the concealed and the revealed." "Concealed" here hints at *Ayin*, while "revealed" hints at *Yesh*, for it is the fusion of *Yesh* with *Ayin* and *Ayin* with *Yesh*. (1:1)

Now Levi Yitzchak shifts into yet another mode of instruction. In Jewish mystical tradition, since God created the world with words ("And God spoke... And there was..."), letters too are primary elements of being. And as such we may assume that their arrangement in words is not accidental. For many moderns the logic initially seems tortured, but in truth it is probably no more preposterous than paying meticulous attention to a Freudian slip or trying to make statements about everyday reality based on particle physics.

To appreciate his argument, we shall need to know two Hebrew words and an alternative way of reading the words of sacred text, known as *ahtbash*. The first is the word for sacred deed, *mitzvah*, מצוה. The second word is the four-letter, ineffable Name of God, spelled *yod, hey, vav,* and *hey.* (Indeed, it is so sacred that we will not even write it out here.)

Ahtbash is a system of letter rearrangement wherein the first letter of the alphabet, *aleph,* is replaced with the last letter, *tav*—hence, *aht*—and the second letter, *bet,* is exchanged with the second from the last letter, *shin*—hence, *bash,* and so on. *Ahtbash* thus opens a new dimension of possible meanings for every word. If this strikes the modern reader as strange, we must remember that Jewish mystics understand letters as ultimate reality awaiting only human interpretive creativity. If the letters of the words in question originate with God—as is assumed to be the case with all the words of Scripture and other sacred traditional texts—then such close readings are eminently reasonable and appropriate.

In the same way the word for sacred deed, *mitzvah,* spelled *mem, tsadi, vav, hey*—according to the alphabetical rearrangement system of *ahtbash*—the letter *mem* becomes *yod,* and the letter *tsadi* becomes *hey* [together pronounced as *Yah,* which is the [first syllable of the ineffable] Name of God, *Yah-veh,* and in this way, the word *mitzvah* becomes *yod, hey, vav, hey.* The *yod hey,* the first half of the word *mitzvah,* represents *Ayin,* and the *vav hey,* the latter half of the word *mitzvah,* represents *Yesh.* And, just as God as *Ayin* is concealed, so the first two letters of the word *mitzvah* likewise conceal the *yod* and *hey* of God's ineffable Name.

And just this is what is meant by what is concealed and what is revealed in *mitzvah:* We perform sacred deeds to bring pleasure to God but [how] it happens remains a mystery to us whereas when we do good deeds for ourselves, it is revealed to us. And this is also how to understand Deuteronomy 29:29, "The secret things belong to the Lord our God..." The "secret things" here refer to what is concealed in the sacred deeds we perform—they belong to the Lord our God, since what we accomplish through them are hidden from us. The "revealed things," on the other hand, as we are instructed in Deuteronomy, "are for us and our children." How we bring such abundance [to ourselves] is revealed to us.

And this finally is the meaning of "In the beginning God created..." It means that the Holy One created *Yesh,* something, which is *reishit* (pronounced ray-SHEET) (the beginning). And only by means of this could come the creation of "heaven and earth," since before the creation there was only *Ayin.* As we read in [the Jerusalem] Talmud's translation, "With wisdom God created..." Wisdom is *Yesh,* some-thingness [of creation]. (1:1)

7.   God is God and there is nothing else.
—Deuteronomy 4:35

הוא האלהים אין עוד מלבדו

Hu ha-Elohim ein od milvado

It's All God

Yitzchak Isaac HaLevi Epstein of Homel, *"Hanah Ariel,"* in *Seeker of Unity*[4]

Surely the most daring, but also the most accurate, way to describe a God who is the ground of all being, the One who continuously brings all creation into being, is with a radical monism: It's all One and it's all God. The assertion of God's unity now takes on new meaning. No longer a mere rejection of polytheism or even an assertion of the unity of God, it now means that all creation—even though anyone can see that the world seems to be broken into myriad discordant parts—is really one. Such thinking permits a mystical reading of Deuteronomy 4:35. Customarily rendered as "The Lord alone is God, there is none beside Him," the Hebrew, *hu ha-Elohim ein od milvado,* also legitimately supports another translation: "The Lord is God, and besides God there is nothing else!" This ecstatic, primal monism is also potentially heretical. If it's all God, then the distinctions upon which so much classical religion is constructed—holy and profane, life and death, and even good and evil—are also dissolved into the divine unity.

The following excerpt is taken from a letter written by one of the early Hasidic masters, Rabbi Yitzchak Isaac Epstein of Homel (1780–1857). It appears in the appendix of Louis Jacobs' *Seeker of Unity.* Jacobs has translated it from the original Hebrew (which is customarily reserved for holy words) and Yiddish (which was the vernacular and used for more informal and secular expression). He has retained, in italics, whatever was originally written in Yiddish; the translations enclosed in single brackets are his own.

Listen, please, my beloved friend! *Nit zog has ve-shalom as dos is apikorsus u-philosophia.* [Do not say that this is, God forfend, heresy and philosophy.] *Rak zog dos is* [Rather say that it is] true belief by virtue of which the dead are revived, so that the dry bones *zollen margish zein* [should experience] the living God. *Un alle Hasidim* [And all Hasidim], especially the disciples of our lord, master and teacher [Schneor Zalman], his soul is in Eden, *hoben die emunah* [have this belief]. *Un sie vert dehort al pi rov in Shemonah 'Esreh.* [And it is generally sensed when reciting the Eighteen Benedictions.] That is to say, after all the goodly meditations while reciting the Songs of Praise and reading the *Shema,* with the higher and lower unification [[see section 8 below]] *vert noch dem dehort* [there is then sensed that], in Yiddish, *altz is Gott* [all is God]. *Un hosekh de-qelipoth Nogah shteht fun veiten un hort vie die velt is a velt un ess shat gor nit un is gor nit mevalvel die menunah.* [And the darkness of the shell of *Noga* [[the broken shards of creation, see section 38]] stands from afar and senses that the world is a world and this does no harm and in no way confuses the belief.] (160)

8. Upper unity, lower unity

יחודא עילאה, יחודה תתאה

Yichuda iela-ah, yichuda tata-ah

Uniting Upper and Lower Worlds

Shneur Zalman of Liady,
Tanya, Sha'ar ha-Yichud veha-Emunah, ch. 7

If ultimate reality is the divine unity, then why does it seem so complex, contradictory, and broken? Any fool can see that the world is not "one." This is one of the abiding problems of all mysticism: If the world is one, then why can't we see it? How are we to reconcile the mystic intuition of an underlying, oceanic Nothingness with the experience of our senses?

Perhaps the most elegant solution is simply that this is precisely the ultimate human endeavor: to make the higher unity of God real, here in this everyday world. The following passage comes from the *Tanya*. (The name, as is frequently the case, comes from the first word in the book.) Its formal title is *Likkutei Amarim* ("Collected Sayings") or *Sefer shel Beinonim* ("The Book of Those Who Are Neither Wholly Good nor Wholly Bad"). It was written by Shneur Zalman of Liady (1747–1813), the founder of Chabad, or Lubavitch Hasidism; he was also known simply as the *Alter Rebbe* ("Old Rebbe"). The book appeared in 1796 and represents the first attempt to systematize a Hasidic theology. It has attained almost canonical status among Lubavitch Hasidim. Lubavitch is one of the most important of the surviving Hasidic dynasties, as well as one of the largest and most geographically dispersed.

Our selection comes from the second of five sections and examines God's relationship to the world. Here we have a concise and elegant description of Shneur Zalman's acosmism (All Being exists within the Divine) and radical monism (It's all One). God practices a continuous and deliberate divine self-concealment! That is why God is hidden from our physical senses. The reality of the world is an illusion. The only true reality is the divine unity. This is also true of one's self; on the highest levels of awareness even the self is dissolved into the divine All.

Shneur Zalman employs another system of letter substitution based on an even more esoteric "mystical grammar." Here the author permits himself to exchange any letters from the same grammatical category with one another. Again, as we saw with Levi Yitzchak's use of *ahtbash* in section 6, our concern is more with the teacher's conclusions than with the process by which he reaches them.

> And so it is understood... according to the *Zohar* (I:18b) that the *Shema* ["Hear O Israel, the Lord our God, the Lord is One *(echad)*" Deuteronomy 6:4] is speaking of a unity on High while the *Barukh shem kevod* ["Blessed be His Name whose glorious kingdom is forever and ever *(va-ed)*," the line that follows the *shema* in the prayer book] speaks of a unity that is below. This is because, according to the system of letter exchange, the word *va-ed* [the last word of the second phrase] is the same as the word *echad* [the last word of the first phrase].

According to *Zohar* II:134a, the letters of the Hebrew alphabet are grouped by their source in the vocal apparatus and the letters in each group are interchangeable. *Aleph, hey, vav,* and *yod* are in one group, so that the *aleph* can be exchanged with *vav. Aleph, hey, chet,* and *ayin* are another group, enabling us to interchange *chet* with *ayin.* In this way, e*chad* (One) literally becomes *va-ed* (forever).

Indeed, the cause and the reason for this *tsimtsum* (God's self-withdrawal) and concealment is that the Holy One of Being concealed and hid the life-force of the world in order that the world would *appear* as a discrete entity with independent existence. Everyone knows that the whole purpose of the creation of the world was for the revelation of God's kingdom. "There can be no king without a people." [Which is to say, it is our role as subjects to make God's kingship real in the world.] (162)

And this is [also] the meaning of the exchanging [of the letters] of the word *Adnut* (Lordship—a lower level Name of God) with the letters of the ineffable, four-letter Name of God *(Havayah)* because this Name of *Havayah* teaches that it is beyond time, that God "was, is and will be" simultaneously—as is written in *Rayah Mehemna* (*Zohar* III:275b, *s.v. parashat Pinhas*). So also is God beyond space because God continually brings into being all dimensions of space, from above to below, and in every direction.

But even though God is beyond space and time, nevertheless God is still manifest spatially and temporally even here below, which is to say that God [the unknowable unity of all Being] unites with God's *Malkhut* [God's spatial and temporal "Kingdom" here below], for from [this unification] space and time are drawn forth and brought into being. Just this is the lower unity [understood by the interchange of letters in God's Ineffable Name of Being,

Havayah, with those of God's Name of *Adnut*]. This is to say that God's being and essence, may it be blessed, is referred to by the Name *Ayn Sof* (without end). God actually fills the whole world in time and space. This is because in the heavens above and on the earth [below] and in every direction, everything is filled with the Light of *Ayn Sof.* [It is] actually the same on the earth below as in the heavens above. This is because all [the heavens and the earth] are within the dimension of space which is nullified within the being of the Light of *Ayn Sof* which clothes itself in God's lowest level of manifestation, the *sefirah* of *Malkhut,* which is united in God.

The *sefirah* of *Malkhut* is also the principle of *tsimtsum* (self-withdrawal) and concealment [and its purpose is] to hide the Light of *Ayn Sof* so that it does not completely annihilate time and space from being so that there be nothing at all—no time or space within being—even here in the lower worlds. (163–164)

The Holy One of Being is simply One without any parts or dimensions whatsoever. And if this be so, then God's being, God's essence and God's knowing are actually all One and without any parts. And therefore, just as it is impossible for any earthly creature to comprehend the being and essence of the Creator, so it is impossible to comprehend the being of God's knowing except to have faith that God is beyond understanding and comprehension. This is because the Holy One of Being is One and unique. God and what God knows are effectively all One. Through God's self-knowledge, God recognizes and knows all being—higher worlds and lower ones even to a little worm in the sea to a tiny gnat in the center of the earth. Nothing is concealed from God. But this knowledge does not add, complicate or multiply God's unity in any way because this is only knowledge of God's self and God's being and God's knowing are all One. (165)

9. Something from Nothing

יש מאין
Yesh mei-Ayin

The Work of Tsaddikim

Dov Baer of Mezritch, *Maggid Devarav Le-Yaakov*[5]

We conclude our consideration of mystic Nothingness with two extraordinary observations by one of the greatest teachers of Nothing in all Jewish tradition, Dov Baer of Mezritch (1704–1772). In the first, Dov Baer, almost mischievously, plays with the work of a spiritual master in contrast to God's work in creating the world. In the second, he turns to how such thinking might function in the process of our own self-transformation. First, some historical background.

We have already read a few passages from Hasidic literature. Hasidism began in eighteenth-century Poland as a folk spiritual revival. It emphasized the importance of joy, fervor, and even ecstasy. The persona of the rabbi was elevated to a kind of spiritual guru who, it was believed, enjoyed frequent intimacy with God. Such rabbis were called rebbes or *tsaddikim* (righteous ones) by the Hasidim, who might routinely travel hundreds of miles to spend a Sabbath once a year in the holy presence of their rebbe. In some dynasties it was believed that the rebbe's intimacy with God also gave him the capacity to work wonders.

The progenitor of it all was a faith healer, storyteller, and charismatic named Israel ben Eliezer, who, because he was particularly effective at invoking the Name of God, came to be known as the Baal Shem Tov ("Master of the Name for Good"), or, as he is more commonly known, the BeSHT (an acronym formed by his initials). Since he wrote virtually nothing, our knowledge of his teaching comes through the writing of his students. The greatest—and most radical—was Dov Baer, the Maggid ("preacher") of Mezritch, or simply "The Great *Maggid*."

Dov Baer, a young scholar of Talmud and Kabbalah, visited the BeSHT and later reported, "He taught me the language of the birds!" Upon of the death of his master, Dov Baer settled in the town of Mezritch in the Ukraine. There he taught the students who would become the third generation of Hasidic leadership: Levi Yitzchak of Berditchev, Menachem Mendl of Vitebsk, Menachem Nachum Twersky of Chernobyl, Ze'ev Wolf of Zhitomir, Aaron of Karlin, Shneur Zalman of Liady, and Chaim Heikl of Amdur. In Mezritch they learned the Great *Maggid*'s doctrine of acosmism: God is the continuous and only source of being; everything else is an illusion; only "Nothingness" can describe such a God. This Nothingness was both psychological and theological. To comprehend the One of Nothing, you must realize that you are its manifestation and therefore nothing yourself!

The following passage comes from the *Maggid*'s principal book, *Maggid Devarav Le-Yaakov*. (The title, as is common with many Hasidic books, is itself lifted from the Bible, in this case Psalm 147:19—"God spoke His words to Jacob." It cleverly evokes the author's name; the last Hebrew letter of each word spells the name "Dov.") Our text is a kind of theological sleight of hand, playing with a theological concept technically called creation *ex nihilo*, "from out of nothing." Tractate *Ketubot* 5a says that the deeds of the *tsaddikim*, the righteous ones (which the Hasidim assumed also referred to their rebbes), are greater than the creation of the heavens and the earth. Commenting on this passage, Dov Baer of Mezritch explains:

> The creation of the heavens and the earth was the bringing
> forth of something from Nothing, but the deeds of the right-

eous ones make Nothing from something. Through everything they do—even ordinary physical things like eating—the righteous raise the holy sparks in the food and thus transform something back into nothing. (sec. 9)

10. Attaining the level of Nothingness

לבוא למדריגת אין

Lavo le-madreigaht Ayin

Transformation

Dov Baer of Mezritch, *Maggid Devarav Le-Yaakov*[6]

Finally, we ponder the implications of such thinking for everyday life and psychology. Dov Baer offers a metaphor for how we might understand the value—and potential danger—of an experience of Nothingness. For the Great *Maggid*, it's the only way to become a new person.

> Nothing is able to change from one form to another—for example, an egg that would hatch into a chick, without first completely nullifying its present form, which is to say, the egg. Only then will another form be able to come forth from it. It is this way with everything in the world: it must attain the level of *Ayin*, Nothingness. Then it will be able to become something else. (sec. 30)

He goes on to suggest that such Nothingness is the necessary source not only of change but of all miracles. The matriarch Sarah's miraculous birth of Isaac required first that she ascend to the highest order of Being, which is *Ayin*, or Nothingness. Indeed, her name change by adding the Hebrew letter *hey* (Genesis 17:15) is itself a metaphor for just such an experience.

So it was with all the miracles that were supernatural, first they needed to attain the tenth and highest *sefirah* of *Ayin,* nothingness. And from there they could influence the form of the miracle. The *RaMBaN* (Moses Nachmanides) notes that God added the letter *hey* to her name, Sarai, making it Sarah, for there was a need that she first ascend to God (whose Name is also abbreviated with the letter *hey*) in order that she could miraculously give birth to Isaac. (sec. 30)

3

Name

A name is more than a word by which we identify something or someone. A name also reveals the essence of its possessor. To know someone's name is to know what makes him tick, what makes her the way she is. And the Name of God is the source of all identities.

When Moses first encounters God at the burning bush, he asks for God's Name. God's reply, "*Ehyeh asher ehyeh,* I will be who I will be," effectively says that God's Name, the essence of all Being, is a moving target. And any attempt to freeze Being by uttering or writing the Name of God is not only blasphemous but impossible. Jewish mystics have therefore resorted to their own euphemisms for the Divine that are equally slippery. As we have seen in the preceding sections, Nothingness is perhaps the closest we can come to saying anything about God. For this reason, of all God's mystical Names, the Name of Nothing is primary.

Before we discuss some of God's Names, we must consider what is unquestionably the most important Jewish mystical text of all time. Indeed, for generations of Jews, it has been as important as the Talmud itself!

11. One Without End
אֵין סוֹף
Ayn Sof

No Borders, No Parts

Zohar II:239a

The *Zohar* (which means "radiance" or" splendor") was written in the northeastern Spanish province of Castile at the end of the thirteenth century by Moses ben Shem Tov de Leon. Fearing that his masterwork would not be accepted by his contemporaries, de Leon claimed that he had discovered a long-lost work of the great second-century mystic Shimon bar Yochai. The core text of the *Zohar* purports to be the faithful transcript of the peripatetic teachings and adventures of Shimon bar Yochai and his students as they walked the Galilee. A collection of perhaps dozens of different commentaries and midrashim (see section 17), the *Zohar* is actually a commentary on the Torah. Scholars today now speak of "Zoharic literature" rather than a single set of books. The *Zohar* is traditionally printed in three volumes: (1) Genesis, (2) Exodus, and (3) Leviticus, Numbers, and Deuteronomy. The Roman numeral in Zoharic citations refers to the volume, the Arabic numeral is the page, and the letter *a* or *b* refers to the folio side— that is, the first side of the page or the second side.

The following passage comes from *Zohar* II:239a. This teaching is not technically about God's actual Name but, perhaps more accurately, God's ultimate kabbalistic euphemism—*Ayn Sof,* the "Infinite One" or the "One Without End." *Ayn Sof* is beyond human comprehension, unknowable. Like the Nothingness discussed above, it is the concealed font of all being.

> He [Rabbi Shimon] said to him [Rabbi Eleazar]: We have been
> taught that [human will] rises up all the way to the *Ayn Sof*

[the One Without End]. For all fusion, unity, and fulfillment are hidden within that hiddenness, unknowable, incomprehensible, the will of all wills. *Ayn Sof* cannot be known; it has neither end nor beginning, unlike the primordial *Ayin* [Nothingness], which does generate a beginning and an end.

What kind of beginning [are we talking about]? A supernal point [an Einsteinian singularity] that is the beginning of everything concealed. Within it arises thought. Even as it brings about the end, as we read in Ecclesiastes 12:13, "The end of the matter." Nevertheless, *Ayn Sof* is still there.

No wills, no lights, no sparks within that *Ayn Sof.* Yet all those sparks and lights depend upon it for their existence even though they do not comprehend. The One who knows and does not know is none other than the ultimate will, concealed within all secrets, *Ayin.* And when the supernal point and the world to come arise, they will know only the aroma, like a traveler passing among fragrances who in turn becomes fragrant.

12. The Name of Being, the Ineffable Name
שם הויה / שם המפורש
Shem Havayah, Shem ha-Meforash

Ten Utterances Contain All
Zohar II:90b

There are myriad mystical names for God. The mystics commonly refer to the name of God's Name as the *Shem Havayah* (the Name of Being) or, sometimes, the *Shem ha-Meforash* (the Explicit Name, the Ineffable Name). This Name is made up of the three Hebrew letters *yod, hey, vav,* and another *hey* (and often incorrectly transliterated as Yahweh). These three letters, in addition to functioning primarily as vowel sounds in unvocalized Hebrew, are also the root letters of the Hebrew verb "to be." Scholars suggest that the Name originally might have meant something like "The One who brings into being all that is."

This Name is also rolled into the kernel of the Sinaitic revelation, the ten utterances, God's self-disclosure.

> Rabbi Eleazar taught: In these ten utterances are encoded all the commandments of the Torah—decrees and punishments, cleanness and uncleanness, branches and roots, trees and plants, heaven and earth, sea and the deeps.
>
> For the Torah is the Name of the Holy One. And just as the Name of the Holy One is encoded in the ten utterances, so the Torah also is encoded in the ten utterances. These ten utterances, they are the Name of the Holy One. And the entire Torah is one Name, the actual sacred Name of the Holy One of Being.

13. The entire Torah is composed of Names of God

התורה כולה שמותיו של קוב"ה

Ha-Torah kula shemotav shel Kudsha Barikh Hu

Torah as Names of God

Moses ben Nachman (Nachmanides), *Commentary on the Torah*[1]

While some Jewish mystics may have been reticent to popularize their theology, the vast majority have taken active roles within the work of their larger Jewish communities. A prime example is Rabbi Moses ben Nachman (1194–1270)—also known as Nachmanides and as the Ramban (an acronym formed by his initials)—from the Spanish city of Gerona. In addition to being a Kabbalist, Nachmanides was also a philosopher, biblical commentator, and leading talmudic scholar (his legal writings are considered classics of rabbinic literature). He was highly influential within Jewish public life in Catalonia. He was once compelled by King Jaime to enter a formal and public theological debate with an apostate Jew, and while the disputation ended in a victory for Nachmanides, the Dominicans subsequently had him tried for attacking Christianity. After interventions—first by the king on Nachmanides' behalf and then by the pope on behalf of the Church, Nachmanides was granted an indefinite postponement but was compelled to flee to Israel. By the end of his life, Nachmanides was widely respected as one of the great Kabbalists of his generation. By the fourteenth century his mystical writings had attained a status on par with the *Zohar* itself.

As we shall consider in sections 16 and 17, in the Jewish mystical tradition the Torah is far more than merely a record of the revelation at Sinai. It is an instrument of creation and a manifestation of the Divine. Similarly, we see in the selection below that the entire Torah is itself a mystical Name of God.

Perhaps one of the most mysterious and baffling of God's Names is the 72-letter Name of God. Technically, it should be called the 216-letter Name of God. If you count the number of Hebrew letters in Exodus 14:19, 20, and 21, you will (or should be) surprised to discover that each verse has 72 letters. The statistical probability of such a repeating string is, needless to say, very, very remote. Kabbalists take these three verses, stack them one on top of another, and then try to pronounce the whole thing by reading the first three letters down, the second three letters up, and so on, until all 216 letters have been pronounced. Professor Joseph Dan of the Hebrew University in Jerusalem has suggested that, in so doing, the Kabbalists have effectively pushed meaningful pronunciation and language beyond the breaking point. We are left only with raw, unmodulated sound. Indeed, perhaps only something so radical could ultimately be the Name of the One of all Being.

> We have a mystical tradition [*kabbalah shel emet; Zohar* II:87a] that the Torah is composed entirely of divine Names and that from another perspective the words [can be seen so as to] separate themselves into [divine] Names. Imagine, for example, that the spaces separating the first three words of the first verse in Genesis can be moved [without adding, deleting, or rearranging any letters] so as to spell an entirely different, yet equally true, statement. And, without even considering other ways [more mystical techniques such as rearranging letters or reinterpretation through their numerical equivalents] for discovering divine names, it is this way with the whole Torah.
>
> And already, our Rabbi Shelomo [Rashi] has written in his commentary on the Talmud about the Great Divine Name of seventy-two letters, which comes from three consecutive verses in Exodus [14:19–21]: "And he went," "And he came," and "And he stretched out." For this reason, a scroll of the Torah with so much as one mistakenly added or deleted letter (even though the letter is only part of a vowel and the word could be written either way without changing the meaning) is disqualified! This principle requires us to disqualify a Torah scroll lacking so much as one letter *vav* from the word *otam [aleph, vav, tav, mem]* which is spelled that way thirty-nine times in the Torah, or *with* the letter *vav* in the same word in myriad other instances when the word appears without it! And so it is in similar situations even though, when one thinks about it, this would seem to make no difference whatsoever. And this is the reason biblical scholars detail every

instance of words spelled with and without an optional vowel letter [like a *vav, yod,* or *hey*] in the Torah and the [rest of the] Bible.

They have compiled books enumerating such irregularities going all the way back to Ezra the scribe and the prophet [according to *Megillah* 15a, Malachai the prophet was Ezra]. We too should be very careful here, as they have interpreted Nehemiah 8:8, "They read from the scroll of the Torah of God, translating it and giving the sense, so that they understood the reading." [According to *Nedarim* 37b, "They read" means the written text; "translating it" means the translation; "giving the sense" alludes to dividing the verses; "so that they understood" refers to the accentuation, but others interpret it as meaning care with regard to the *mesorah,* or variant spellings.]

It appears that the Torah is written in black fire on white fire [Jerusalem Talmud, *Shekalim* 13b; Midrash *Tanchuma* on Genesis 1:1; Rashi on Deuteronomy 33:2] in this regard, [so all the words] were therefore written continuously without any spaces between them. And this means that it is possible then to read it both the way we normally read it as teaching or commandment and as Divine Names. It was given to Moses, our teacher, so that it could be read as [a document of] commandments, but it was also transmitted orally as Divine Names.

Thus, as I have mentioned, [the Kabbalists] would write the letters of the Great [seventy-two-letter] Name of God successively without spaces. [Writing each of the three verses from Exodus 14 in three rows, stacked one on top of another] they would then subdivide it into three-letter words [read first down and then up as well as many other divisions as is done by the masters of Kabbalah. (6–7)

14. Let him kiss me with the kisses of his mouth. —Song of Songs 1:2

ישקני מנשיקות פיהו

Yishakeni mi-neshikot pi-hu

The loss of self that results from the experience of oceanic Nothingness we have already discussed is similar, if not identical, to the loss of self felt in the rapture of love. Both are metaphors frequently employed by mystics of all traditions. Not only does love offer us heightened sensitivity to our world and own innermost experience, but love and spiritual ecstasy both involve the temporary dissolution of one's borders. Indeed, the French word for *orgasm* is *petit mort,* "little death." In the mystic union, we "die *unto*" God. It is a death from which we are reborn.

Rabbi Adin Steinsaltz, the great contemporary Israeli talmudic scholar and mystic (see section 34), has wisely noted in commenting on the Song of Songs that love of God is pale in contrast to the physical passion of one earthly lover for another, whereas physical love without some transcendent spiritual yearning is simply boring.

The two hymns below, still widely sung as part of the Sabbath liturgy, easily move back and forth between religious and romantic, spiritual and physical, imagery. Their enduring popularity testifies to the continued power and wisdom of the metaphors themselves.

Lekha Dodi *("Come, My Beloved")*
Shelomo Ha-Levi Alkabetz, in the Daily Prayerbook

We know few details of the life of the Kabbalist and poet Shelomo Alkabetz (c. 1505–1584). He settled in Safed and became an active player in the Lurianic kabbalistic revival of that time (see section 38). Alkabetz relates how on the night of Shavuot, while he was studying Torah with his friend Joseph Caro, author of the

Shulchan Arukh, the great code of Jewish law, a *maggid,* a divine muse, appeared to Caro. The two friends therefore decided to establish a custom of staying awake on the night of Shavuot to study the Torah. They called their practice a *tikkun leil Shavuot,* a "making ready for the night of receiving Torah." The custom is still widely practiced today.

Alkabetz probably also initiated the custom of dressing in white and going out at sunset into the fields on the outskirts of town to welcome the Sabbath with a recital of hymns and Psalms 95 through 99. The ritual came to be known as *Kabbalat Shabbat,* welcoming the Sabbath (bride). His hymn *Lekha Dodi* ("Come, My Beloved") achieved unparalleled popularity (there are hundreds of melodies) and is sung in Jewish communities on Friday evenings. The hymn sings of a longing for redemption and the divine presence. It imagines a cosmic union between God the groom and Shabbat the bride, with the people of Israel serving as attendants.

The hymn is also an acrostic—the first Hebrew letters of each verse spell the author's first names, Shelomo Ha-Levi. Like much Jewish mystical literature it is staggeringly rich with biblical and talmudic allusions. These are noted. Like the literature of sixteenth-century Safed, the hymn is also intricate with alphabetical and numerical mystical associations. To give just one example (I am grateful to Professor Reuven Kimelman of Brandeis University for calling this to my attention), the Hebrew of the first line has fifteen letters, which correspond to the numerical equivalent of the first two letters, *yod* and *hey,* of God's Ineffable Name; the second line has eleven letters, corresponding to the last two letters, *vav* and *hey,* of the Name. We realize, upon closer scrutiny, that the hymn itself is only the surface of a multilayered expression of piety and love.

Jewish mystics, like their counterparts in all traditions, are drawn to romantic imagery in their attempt to describe their experience. Eros awakens us to a heightened sensuality toward the world and simultaneously enables us to go beyond our individual

selves as we seek to serve the one we love. In love, the two again
become one. Here the lovers are God and God's exiled feminine
presence—the *Shekhinah* (see section 21), who is with the people
of Israel and the Sabbath.

> Come, my lover, let us meet the bride,
> Let us receive the presence of Shabbat.
>
> "Keep Shabbat"[a] and "Remember Shabbat"[b]
> Our God proclaimed both in the same utterance!
> God is one and God's Name is one,
> Incredible, wondrous, and awesome.
>
> Come, let us go to meet Shabbat,
> For indeed she is the source of blessing.
> Anointed from the beginning of time,
> The last thing created yet the first conceived.[c]
>
> Temple of the King in the royal city;
> Arise, come forth from your desolation.[d]
> Long enough have you dwelt in the valley of tears;
> Now let God dower you with love.[e]
>
> Shake off the dust, arise![f]
> Put on the splendid clothes of my people.
> Through the power of the son of Jesse of Bethlehem;
> My soul's redemption draws near.
>
> Awaken, O awaken yourself;[g]
> Your light begins to shine, grow brighter![h]
> Now rise and sing your song;[i]
> God's presence through you revealed.

Don't be embarrassed; don't be ashamed; [j]
Why are you dejected? Why are you sad?[k]
The afflicted of my people will gather within you;
The city shall be rebuilt on her ancient ruins.[l]

Those who tried to devour you
shall themselves be devoured;[m]
All your tormentors shall be scattered!
Your God will rejoice over you
Like a bridegroom rejoicing over his bride.[n]

You will spread forth in every direction;[o]
Stand in reverence before God.
Through the power of the one
who is the son of Peretz;[p]
Let us be happy and rejoice.[q]

Come in peace, her husband's crown;
Yes, in joy and exaltation.
Into the midst of the faithful of your precious people;
Come O bride! Come to us now!

a. Deuteronomy 5:12, "Observe the Sabbath day and keep it holy."
b. Exodus 20:8, "Remember the Sabbath day and keep it holy."
c. Talmud, *Pesachim* 54a.
d. Talmud, *Shabbat* 118b.
e. Jeremiah 15:5, "But who will pity you, O Jerusalem?"
f. Isaiah 52:2, "Arise, shake off the dust; Sit [on your throne], Jerusalem!
g. Isaiah 51:17, "Rouse, rouse yourself! Arise, O Jerusalem."

h. Isaiah 60:1, "Arise, shine for your light has dawned."

i. Judges 5:12, "Awake, awake, strike up the chant!"

j. Isaiah 54:4, "You shall not be shamed, do not cringe."

k. Psalms 42:12, "Why so downcast, my soul, why disquieted within me?"

l. Jeremiah 30:18, "The city shall be rebuilt on its mound."

m. Jeremiah 30:16, "Those who despoiled you shall be despoiled."

n. Isaiah 62:5, "And as a bridegroom rejoices over his bride, so will your God rejoice over you."

o. Isaiah 54:3, "For you shall spread out to the right and to the left."

p. Genesis 38:29, "So he was named Peretz"; Ruth 4:18–22, "This is the line of Peretz...Jesse begot David."

q. Isaiah 25:9, "Let us rejoice and exult in His deliverance."

Yedid Nefesh *("O Love of My Soul")*

Eleazar ben Moses Azikri, in the Daily Prayerbook

Eleazar ben Moses Azikri (1533–1600) of Safed was the author of *Sefer Haredim*, a comprehensive volume on Jewish ethics that, along with Elijah de Vidas's *Reishit Chokhmah* (see section 45) served as the basis for Jewish pietism of the seventeenth and eighteenth centuries and helped to popularize kabbalistic thought.

The goals of this ascetic were spiritual perfection *(tikkun)*, purification *(taharah)*, and communion *(devekut)* with God. He divided his day between writing and meditation. During the latter time he would not even study but would only sit in reverent silence without moving his eyes. With two colleagues, Azikri drafted articles of spiritual partnership. Together, they and the members of their small group pledged themselves to refrain from worldly activity and, instead, to devote all their time to Torah study and prayer. Their explicit goals included loving others, not judging them, thinking continually about God, and praying with devotion. Members of the group did not accept any public function, nor did they officiate as rabbis.

One of their love poems to God, originally published in Azikri's *Sefer Haredim*, is *Yedid Nefesh*. This *piyyut*, or liturgical poem, has been accepted throughout the Jewish world and appears just before the *Kabbalat Shabbat* ("Welcoming the Sabbath") liturgy in all Sefardi (Spanish-Portuguese and Middle Eastern)—and increasingly in Ashkenazi (German and East European)—prayer books to this day.

> O Love of my soul, Father of Womb;
>> draw me to Your want,
> I can run like a deer;
>> reverent toward Your presence,
> Your love so soft;
>> even sweeter than liquid honey.
>
> Radiant brightness of Being;
>> my soul, faint with Your yearning,
> O God of seeking, heal her;
>> show her the ecstasy of Your light.
> Then at last recovery and vigor;
>> now Your servant and forever.
>
> O God, Your longing intimacy;
>> easy please for a child You love,
> I am only this endless waiting and wanting;
>> just to peek Your Presence,
> Please God, my heart's desire;
>> hurry now with no more hiding.

Show me here Your love;
    cover me with the shade of Your time.
Your presence lighting the sky;
    a wedding feast of Your joy,
Hurry now my darling, the time is here;
    loving like long, long ago.

Part Two

The Torah of God is really very simple.
—PSALM 19:8

4

Truth

It is impossible to overestimate the importance of Torah in Jewish mysticism. In traditional Judaism, of course, Torah has always been the word of God, but for Jewish mystics it is even more. The Torah scroll—its pericopes and spaces, even the very letters themselves—becomes nothing less than a manifestation *of* God.

Gershom Scholem, the master historian of Jewish mysticism, is unequivocal:

> The acceptance of the Torah, in the strictest and most precise understanding of the concept of the word of God, in other words...Torah from heaven...[is the] basic assumption upon which all traditional Jewish mysticism in Kabbalah and Hasidism is based.[1]

Such a notion, that the Torah is a manifestation of ultimate truth, not only strains the credulity of many modern (and probably all liberal) readers, but also has apparently been a stretch for Jews for centuries. The antidote to our religious skepticism may begin with romance. In the fourteenth century, the *Zohar* offered the following teaching (section 15). In it, the author invites us to recall our own experience of love and romance and, with it, our heightened awareness and our resultant ability to pay close attention to otherwise seemingly trivial details. As we saw in the preceding section, such language of romantic intimacy naturally lends itself to mystical expression.

15. Each day the Torah calls us in love

אורייתא קרי בכל יומא בנהימו

Oraita kerei be-khol yoma bin-himu

Romance and Revelation

Zohar II:99a–b

In this oft-quoted passage, an "old man" is trying to help his students learn how to read Torah. Through metaphor, the Torah "herself" becomes a maiden intent on seducing and revealing herself to her lover. The text coaxes us to recall our own loves, when everything around us was transformed into sensual delight and opportunities for giving to another. In such a way we progress from simple romantic infatuation to an evolved, mystical rapture. The experience of love—first sensual, then selfless—helps us to understand how to receive the gift of God's revelation.

> The old man said: *Chevra*, it's not for this alone that I've begun to speak; an old man like me doesn't just rattle on about one thing and then stop. People are so confused. They don't understand about the truth of Torah. She calls to them every day in love and longing but they won't even turn their heads!
>
> Nevertheless, she unwraps a word, lets it be seen just a little bit, then she quickly hides it away again. But when she does this, revealing a little bit of herself and then immediately concealing herself, it is only for those who would know her and understand her.

This can be understood by a parable. There is a beautiful woman, hidden in her palace. She has a lover. No one else knows; the whole thing is clandestine. And that lover, because of his great longing for her, continually passes the entrance to her palace, looking, waiting. She knows that he is walking back and forth by the entrance.

What does she do? She opens the door of that hidden palace just a little bit and shows her face to him. Then she quickly closes it and hides again. No one else sees or even notices what's going on, only the one who loves her. And his heart and soul, his inner being flow after her. He knows that because of his love for her, she has revealed herself to him for this one moment to awaken him.

It is the same way with a word of Torah. She does not reveal herself except to those who love her. Torah knows that one who is wise passes back and forth in front of her doorway all the time. What does she do? She reveals her face from within her palace by giving him a hint and immediately withdraws to her hiding place. No one else knows what's going on, only he alone. And his heart and soul, his inner being flow after her. In this way Torah reveals and conceals herself; she does what she does to awaken love in her lover.

Come and see. This is the way of Torah. At first, when she begins to reveal herself to a man, she entices him with a hint. If he understands, good. If he doesn't understand, she sends him a message and calls him a fool. Torah says to that messenger, tell that fool to come closer so that I can talk to him. As we read in Proverbs 9:4, "Who is this fool without understanding? Let him come here."

He approaches her. She begins to speak with him from behind a curtain hung in front of him, little by little—words he can gradually comprehend. And this is called *derashah*—seeking, interpretation. Later she speaks with him through a delicate veil, perplexing words. And this is called *aggadah*—narrative, legend.

Finally, once he has become accustomed to her, she reveals herself to him, face to face. She speaks of all her hidden mysteries, all the hidden ways, long ago concealed within her heart. Now he is a complete human being, a husband of Torah, indeed, a master of the house. All her secrets she reveals to him, withholding nothing from him, concealing nothing.

She says to him: Do you remember that first hint I gave you so long ago? So many secrets, here and there. Now he understands why he must not add to those words or take any away. At once it is clear: Even the superficial meaning of the text must be just like it is, without the addition or subtraction of even so much as one letter. For this reason human beings must be ever zealous to pursue Torah, to be her lovers.

We Could Write Better Stories
Zohar III:152a

In another passage, the *Zohar* is even more direct in its acknowledgment of Scripture's *apparent* lack of spiritual depth. Again, we are astonished by the *Zohar*'s ability to anticipate questions we thought were unique to our own contemporary religious situation.

Rabbi Shimon said, woe to those who claim that the Torah comes to only to relate stories of this world in ordinary language. If this were so, even in our time we would be able to use ordinary language and write an even better Torah! Or if you say that it comes to teach affairs of this world, even we have ordinary books that do a better job.

All the words of Scripture conceal supernal truths and awesome secrets.

Come and see: The world above and the world below must be understood as parallel to one another. Israel below and the angels on high. Of the angels it is written in Psalm 104:4, "He makes His angels spirits." But when they descend below, they are clothed in the garments of this world. If this were not so, they would not be able to survive, nor would the world be able to endure their presence. And if it is this way with angels, how much the more so for Scripture, which is the very blueprint for all creation.

In this way a scriptural story must be read as merely an outer garment. Woe to one who imagines that the outer clothing is the actual Scripture, for he will have no portion in the world to come. As David said in Psalm 119:18, "Open my eyes so that I may behold the wonders of Your Torah," beneath the superficial garments.

The Order of the Parshiyot Is Hidden
Midrash Tehillim [Psalms] 3:4

The two passages above suggest that (1) loving Torah opens "her" to us and (2) even apparently simple stories contain infinite meaning. The following midrash goes on to suggest that to the properly educated reader, the Torah might even grant divine powers. However, the true order, and therefore the real meaning, of Torah is concealed from us and known only to God.

Rabbi Eleazar [ben Padat], commenting on Job 28:13: "'No man knows its order,' said that the paragraphs of the Torah were not given in the proper order. For if they were, anyone who read them would at once be able to create the world, resurrect the dead, and perform miracles. For this reason the correct order of the sections of the Torah were hidden and are known only to the Holy One of Being, of whom it is said (Isaiah 44:7): "And who, like Me, can read and proclaim and set it in order for Me?"

16. The whole world is made of letters

כל העולם היא האותיות

Kol ha-olam hi ha-otiyot

God of the Letters

Menachem Nachum Twersky of Chernobyl, *Me'or Eina'im* [2]

Menachem Nachum Twersky of Chernobyl (1730–1789) was a disciple of Dov Baer of Mezritch (see section 9). He lived a life of poverty, even after giving up the life of a schoolteacher to become the "preacher" in Chernobyl. In this brief passage, he speaks of the relationship between the letters of the Hebrew alphabet and the world around us. The "world of speech" *(olam ha-dibbur)*, in addition to its plain meaning, is also an allusion to the *shekhinah*, God's indwelling presence, *Malkhut*, the lowest of the ten *sefirot* (see section 21).

As we recall from the opening chapter of Genesis, God created the world not by physically making it but by speaking it into being. Because the letters of the Hebrew alphabet are the elements of speech, the letters are likewise more than merely signs for sounds or even the primary instruments of God's revelation; they are the very building blocks of reality.

The Holy One created the world with Torah, which is to say, with the twenty-two letters [of the Hebrew alphabet], all creatures were created through the world of speech. (20)

The Letters of God

The Book of [Divine] Unity [3]

The letters of the Hebrew alphabet are even more than the medium of divine communication and the instruments of creation; they are themselves holy. By extension, the letters as they are arrayed in the Torah are effectively the closest we can come to envisioning a God who can have no image. As we read in the words of the anonymous author of *The Book of [Divine] Unity*, the letters on the scroll of a Torah and the "shape" of God are somehow related.

> All the letters of the Torah, by their shapes, combined and separated, swaddled letters, curved ones and crooked ones, superfluous and elliptic ones, minute and large ones, and inverted, the calligraphy of the letters, the open and closed pericopes and the ordered ones, all of them are the shape of God...since if one letter is missing from the Scroll of the Torah, or one is superfluous...that Scroll of the Torah is disqualified, since it has not in itself the shape of God. (145)

The Mystical Body of God

Menachem Recanati [4]

Menachem Recanati, a fourteenth-century Italian Kabbalist, takes this idea of the holiness of the Hebrew letters to its ultimate conclusion:

> The letters [of God's Name and of the Torah] are the mystical body of God, while God, in a manner of speaking, is the soul of the letters. (44)

Lost Letters

Yaakov Yosef of Polnoye, *Toledot Yaakov Yosef* [5]

We conclude our consideration of Torah and its components, the letters of the Hebrew alphabet, with a Hasidic admonition about how to read.

One must, of course, always attempt to read sacred text with the proper devotion. Indeed, to do whatever you do as an extension of the divine will is the goal of all Jewish religious life. Religious deeds may be performed for a variety of intentions—to impress friends, to remind us of our parents, because they're beautiful, because they can do wonderful things for our souls. However, the highest goal is to be fully present in the deed, to transcend one's own motives, to simply be an agent of God's request. This is termed, in Hebrew, to do something *lishmah*, "for its own sake," the ultimate intention.

We have a teaching from Yaakov Yosef of Polnoye (d. 1782), one of the principal disciples of the Baal Shem Tov. In a daring analogy—one that presages postmodernism with its location of meaning not in the text but in the eyes of the reader—Yaakov Yosef elevates the proper reading of Torah to cosmic, even messianic, significance. For him, the sacred text of Scripture is lost and asleep, awaiting our devotions.

It once happened that some travelers lost their way and decided to go to sleep until someone came along who could show them the way. Someone first came along and led them to a place of wild beasts and brigands, but then someone else came and showed them the right path. It is the same way with the letters of the Torah, through which the world was created. They have come to this world in the form of travelers but have lost their way and fallen asleep. When someone comes along, however, and studies Torah for its own sake, *lishmah,* such a one leads them on the right path so that they can cleave with their root. (172)

17. God created the world with the Torah

באורייתא ברא קוב"ה עלמא

B'Oraita bera Kudsha berikh hu alma

The DNA of Creation

Midrash *Genesis Rabbah* 1:1

Midrash is a unique, Jewish literary art form. There is poetry, short story, commentary, novella—and then there is midrash. Midrash is predicated on the reader's presumed close familiarity with the biblical text. Playing on the assumption that you already know the story, and without changing one word of the Bible, midrash suggests other ways to understand the same events and join them to other, often distant, biblical verses. Whereas the goal of commentary would be to further explain and clarify the meaning of Scripture, midrash shamelessly imagines and even concocts whole other layers of narrative and meaning. A good midrash, therefore, will *not* elucidate the intention of the biblical author. On the contrary, it will forever confuse it with other stories. There are scores of anthologies of midrash (indeed, midrash is still being written). The largest and most influential of such collections is *Midrash Rabbah,* based on the Torah and the five scrolls (Song of Songs, Ruth, Lamentations, Ecclesiastes, and Esther). Although midrash is not generally considered to be mystical, the following selections demonstrate how classical religious literature can easily have mystical implications.

The author of the following midrash is fascinated by the Hebrew word *bereishit,* usually rendered as "In the beginning." The Hebrew preposition, *bet,* or "in," can just as easily be translated as "with." In other words, "with *reishit*," God created the world. Perhaps, the midrash suggests, *reishit* means Torah. The midrash proceeds from there to a series of nuanced, punning biblical proof-texts and concludes with its mystical insight.

As we have already seen above, if the letters and words of Torah are manifestations of the Divine, then to read and understand them correctly is to comprehend the ultimate nature of reality itself. For this reason, the Torah is a blueprint for the universe, a kind of DNA of creation. More than an instruction manual for how the world works, the Torah is a diagram for how the world was made.

> "*Bereishit,* in [or with] *reishit* [the beginning] God created the heavens and the earth" (Genesis 1:1). Rabbi Hoshaya opened his teaching by citing Proverbs 8:30, "Then I was with [God] as a confidant, *amon,* daily, a source of delight." *Amon* can also mean "tutor" as well as "covered" and "hidden," and there are those who say *amon* also means "great."
>
> *Amon* means a tutor, as we read in Numbers 11:12, "As an *omein,* a nursing father, carries an infant." *Amon* also means "covered," as we read in Lamentations 4:5, "*He-emunim,* those who were covered in purple." And *amon* can mean "hidden," as we read in Esther 2:7, "And he [Mordecai] raised Hadassah [concealing her true identity]." And *amon* can also mean great, as we read in Nahum 3:8, "Are you better than *No-amon* [an Assyrian deity]?" The rest of this verse can be translated, "Are you better than Alexandria the Great, situated between two rivers?"
>
> Another interpretation of the Genesis text: *Amon* can also be read as *uman,* an artist. The Torah says, "I was the artistic plan of the Holy One." Normally, in our world, when a mortal king builds a palace, he doesn't have the expertise to design it alone; he hires an architect. The architect also

does not build it spontaneously; he uses diagrams and blueprints to know how to make the rooms and the doors. In the same way, the Holy One looked into the Torah and created the world. The Torah said, "*Bereishit,* with *reishit* God created the heavens and the earth." *Reishit* means nothing other than Torah, as we read in Proverbs 8:22, "God made me the beginning of God's way."

18. The sound of almost breathing

קול דממה דקה

Kol demama daka

The Silence of Elijah

1 Kings 19:8–12

We turn now to one of the central problems in Jewish mysticism. How did God, who is infinite, manage to communicate with human beings, who are finite? When the infinite meets the finite, one of them must, by logical necessity, become the other. How, then, could even the holiest document be a manifestation of the Divine? We say, for instance, that God "spoke" as if God had a mouth, tongue, and palate, but if God has no vocal organs, then what does "speak" mean?

Generally, Jewish mystics seem less comfortable with a transcendent divine voice thundering from the heavens than with an immanent one whispering from within. For this reason they are drawn to the quiet revelation experienced by Elijah and describe their own revelations as a *gilui Eliyahu,* revelation of Elijah. We notice at once the unmistakable parallels between the Elijah experience and that of Moses on Sinai. Both were on the same mountain, within the same cave. Both remained there forty days and forty nights. Indeed, the Talmud says they are the same man. For both, there was smoke, lightning, thunder, and earthquake. The singular difference between the two stories is that in the mosaic version, God's voice is loud and the message is unequivocal. In the Elijah version, God speaks from almost total silence.

> And [Elijah] arose and ate and drank and traveled on the strength of that meal for forty days and forty nights until he came to the mountain of God, Horeb. He entered a cave and spent the night. And behold, the word of God came to him and said, "Why are you here, Elijah?" And he replied, "Because I have been very passionate about the Lord, the God of hosts, for the children of Israel have forsaken Your covenant. Your altars they have destroyed, your prophets they have murdered with the sword. Only I am left and they want to kill me, too." So God said, "Go, station yourself on the mountain before the Lord." And behold, the Lord passed by. And before the Lord there was a windstorm so strong that it broke the mountain and shattered rocks; but the Lord was not in the wind. And after the wind, an earthquake; but the Lord was not in the earthquake. And after the earthquake, a firestorm; but the Lord was not in the firestorm. And after the firestorm, the thin, barely audible noise of almost breathing!

The Silence of Sinai
Midrash *Exodus Rabbah* 29:9

The author of the next midrash is also fascinated with this notion of a revelation in silence. The divine voice not only demands silence but also requires it. Any other noise could drown it out. Indeed, our own ability to receive God's word begins with our own capacity to maintain silence. George Eliot said, "If we had a keen vision and feeling for all ordinary human life, it would be like hearing the grass grow, the squirrel's heart beat, and we should die of that roar which lies on the other side of silence."

> "I am the Lord thy God." It is written (in Amos 3:8), "The lion hath roared, who will not fear?" ...Said Rabbi Abbahu in the name of Rabbi Yochanan: When the Holy One gave the Torah no bird screeched, no fowl flew, no ox bellowed, none of the *ofanim* [angels] flapped a wing, the *seraphim* did not say "Holy, holy, holy," the sea did not roar, none of the creatures uttered a sound, throughout the whole world was there was only a deafening silence as the [divine] voice went forth, "I am the Lord thy God."

Two Voices in One

Midrash Exodus Rabbah 5:9

The next midrash considers the multiplicity of meanings in the divine word. In one sense, that is the creative engine in every midrash: to plumb the infinity of meanings necessarily present in the divine word. One tradition, for instance, says that since there were seventy languages, there are seventy faces for each word in the Torah. Another maintains that, since there were 600,000 Jews present at Sinai, there were 600,000 meanings. Such an infinite revelation evokes the logical impossibility of the infinite (God) encountering the finite (human being). Notice also how the author creatively interweaves passages from Exodus, Deuteronomy, Psalms, and Job all into the same fantasy and how, after an artful and free-associative odyssey, we return to the verse from which we began.

> And the Lord said to Aaron: "Go into the wilderness to meet Moses" (Exodus 4:27). It is written in Job, "God thunders marvelously with His voice" (37:5). What does "thunders" mean?

When the Holy One gave the Torah on Sinai, God showed wonders upon wonders to Israel with God's voice. How so? The Holy One spoke, and the Voice reverberated throughout the whole world. Israel heard the Voice coming to them from the south, so they ran to the south to meet the Voice. But from the south, it switched around to the north, so they ran to the north. From the north it shifted to the east, so they ran to the east; but from the east it changed to the west, so they ran to the west. From the west it changed to the heavens. But when they raised their eyes heavenwards, it seemed to proceed from the earth, so they looked back to the earth, as it is said, "From the heavens God let you hear God's voice, to discipline you; and on earth God let you see God's great fire; and from the midst of that fire you heard God's words" (Deuteronomy 4:36). Then the Israelites said to one to another, "But wisdom, where shall it be found?" (Job 28:12)....

It says: "And all the people perceived the thunderings" (Exodus 20:15). The text does not say "thunder," but "thunderings." Rabbi Yochanan explained that God's voice split into seventy voices, in [each one of the] seventy languages [of humanity], in order that all the nations should understand. When each nation heard the Voice in its own mother tongue, they all died, except for Israel, who heard and were not injured.

How did [God's] voice go forth? Rabbi Tanchuma said: The word went out and split in two, killing idolators who would not accept it but giving life to Israel who accepted the Torah. This is what Moses said to them at the end of forty years: "For what mortal ever heard the voice of the living God speak out of the fire, as we did, and lived?" (Deuteronomy 5:23). You have heard God's voice and lived, but the idolators heard it and all died.

Come and see how the Voice went forth to each and every Israelite according to his or her own individual strength—to the old, according to their strength, and to the young, according to theirs; to the children, to the babies and to the women, according to their strength; and even to Moses according to his strength, as it is said, "Moses spoke, and God answered him by a voice" (Exodus 19:19); that means, with a voice that he could endure. Thus it says in Psalm 29:4, "The voice of the Lord is with power," not "with *His* power," but simply "with power"; this means with the power of each individual, even to pregnant women according to their strength. Thus to each person it was according to his or her strength....

From where do we know that the Voice divided itself into many voices so that the people would not be injured? Because it is written in Exodus 20:15, "And all the people perceived the thunderings [and no one was hurt!]." For this reason Job 37:5 says, "God thunders marvelously with His voice."...

Rabbi Reuben said: At the time when God said to Moses in Midian, "Go, return to Egypt" (Exodus 4:19), the utterance was divided into two voices; it was divided in two. Moses heard the Voice in Midian saying, "Go, return to Egypt," but Aaron heard it saying, "Go into the wilderness to meet Moses" (Exodus 4:27). Thus God thunders marvelously with His voice.

In Your Face!

Naftali Tsvi Horowitz of Ropczyce, *Zera Kodesh*[6]

One of the most dazzling mystical reinterpretations of the revelation at Sinai comes to us from Rabbi Naftali Tsvi Horowitz of Ropczyce (1760–1827). He begins with a midrash about what happened at Sinai. There seem to be at least three associations that spark the Ropczycer's teaching. The number 22,000 evokes the twenty-two letters of the Hebrew alphabet; the Hebrew word *alphei*, "thousands," evokes the name of the first letter of the Hebrew alphabet, *aleph*; and the image of God speaking with us "face to face" has been irresistible for generations of Jewish mystics. After quoting the midrash, he cites an extraordinary teaching in the name of his own teacher, Rabbi Mendl of Rymanov, on the real content of the revelation and concludes with a extraordinary image for the construction of an ethical system.

> We read in *Midrash Shemot Rabbah* 29:2: "I am the Lord your God" (Exodus 20:2). It is written, "The Lord spoke with you face to face" (Deuteronomy 5:4). Rabbi Abdimi of Haifa said: Twenty-two thousand [angels] descended with God on Sinai, as it says, "The chariots of God are myriads, even thousands upon thousands; the Lord is among them as in Sinai in holiness" (Psalm 68:18). Note that in the words "the Lord is among them," the Name of God is not written with a *yod* and a *hey* [and a *vav* and a *hey*], but with an *aleph* and a *dalet* [Adonai], to show that the Lord of the whole world was among them. (Rabbi Levi offered another explanation of this: The tablet of the *Shem ha-Meforash* was inscribed on their hearts.)
>
> It seems to me that this can be understood according to something I once heard from the mouth of my revered master and teacher, Rabbi Mendl of Rymanov [1745–1815], his memory is a blessing. He explained the verse in Psalms 62:12, "One thing God has spoken but two things I have heard." It is possible, he taught, that at Sinai we heard nothing from the mouth of God other than the letter *aleph* of the first utterance, "I am the Lord your God" (Exodus 20:2). [The first letter of the first word I, *anokhi*, is *aleph*.] "O how beautiful are the words from the mouth of a sage!" (Ecclesiastes 10:12). And to understand such a holy teaching is like hear-

ing the words of the living God, for His words—"Behold, My Word is like fire, declares the Lord, like a hammer that shatters rock!" (Jeremiah 23:29).

We can now also understand [the apparent contradiction between] the passages in Deuteronomy 5:4, "The Lord spoke with you face to face at the mountain from the midst of the fire" and Deuteronomy 4:15, "You saw no image when the Lord your God spoke to you at Horeb from out of the fire." There was nothing [that could be seen, in other words] but a voice!

It is possible to explain this in the light of a teaching by our sages on Psalm 16:8, "I set the Lord before me continually." They say that this verse represents a great principle of the Torah. One might think they would have said that serving God or something similar was a great principle. It becomes clear when we read it in light of a tradition in our *musar*, or ethical, literature. There we learn that the *Shem ha-Meforash*, the awesome Name of God, the four-letter Name of *yod, hey, vav,* and *hey,* itself actually hints at the letter *aleph* א. For the letter *aleph* itself is constructed of two letter *yods* י [*yod* is the tenth letter of the alphabet, so two add up to 20] with the letter *vav* ו [sixth letter] joining them in the middle. This makes a total of 26. The four-letter Name of God, *yod, hey, vav,* and *hey* [*yod* = 10, *vav* = 6, six and two letter *heys*, each being 5, also] total 26!

This, in turn, hints at the face of a human being. The two eyes resemble two letter *yods*, and a nose between them looks like a letter *vav!* In other words, on every human face there is a letter *aleph!* And just this is the meaning of Genesis 1:27, "In the image of God, [God] created him [the first human]." And this facial aleph, engraved on every person, has the same numerical equivalent, 26, as God's most awesome name, *yod, hey, vav,* and *hey!*

We also know that there is a kind of effulgence [divine light] surrounding every person, just as in holiness we are radiant. And this is the reason we are bidden to continually keep the image of God ever before our faces, for indeed, the seal of the Holy One is literally on our faces, evoking the shape [of the Name] of the Creator. This is what our sages meant when they spoke of a great principle of the Torah. When we were worthy to stand at God's chosen mountain and we heard the voice issuing the letter *aleph*, we were fulfilled and there was revealed to us the shape of the letter *aleph*. As we read in Exodus 20:15, "And all the people saw the thunder." In other words, they saw what was heard [synesthesia]! We saw the form of the letter *aleph*, itself evoking the Name of God. And [at that moment] they all saw and understood that this was also the form of their own faces! And this then is the reason that we read just after the theophany in Exodus 20:17, "Be not afraid; for God has come only in order to test you, and in order that the fear of [God] may be ever with you so that you do not go astray," for when a person continually keeps this idea [that God is in the face of every other human being], then he [or she] will not easily be inclined to go astray. (40a)

19. How to say (your own) Torah

להגיד תורה
Le-hagid Torah

How to Say Torah

Dov Baer of Mezritch, *Or Ha-Meir*[7]

We conclude our consideration of the mystery of Torah with a surprising Hasidic twist. As we have seen, God created the universe with or through the Torah. It is not only the blueprint of creation;

Torah is, as it were, an expression of God's innermost teaching. Among the Hasidim, when the rebbe taught, they would say that the rebbe is "saying Torah." To be sure, the rebbe was expounding on *the* Torah, *God's* Torah, but the phrase also came to mean that the rebbe was giving voice to his own innermost interpretations and teachings. In a similar way we imagine that every teacher—indeed, every person—has his or her unique, innermost teaching, if you will, a torah. This "torah," usually expressed in words, might also be shared in music or dance or any other form of expression.

The following passage comes to us as advice from Dov Baer of Mezritch to his students on how to "say Torah." It is transmitted by one of his students, Zev Wolf of Zhitomir (d. 1798).

> Once I heard [Dov Baer] the *Maggid* say to us: "I will teach you explicitly the best way to say Torah." He was not aware of himself at all but only an ear that hears what the universe of the utterance *[olam ha-dibbur]* is speaking through him, but he himself does not speak, and the moment he begins to hear his own words, he stops.
>
> I beheld this many times, an ordinary event, when he opened his mouth to speak words of Torah, he appeared to everyone as if he were not of this world at all—as if the divine presence were speaking from his throat. And sometimes, even in the middle of a topic or even in the middle of a word, he would stop and pause for a while... (213, col. 2)

5

Organism

Perhaps the central theological problem for all mysticism is simply this: How can God, who is one, make the world, which is many? Its corollary is equally confounding: Why would God bother doing so, anyway? One especially creative and elaborate solution to this problem initiates Jewish mysticism's best-known expression, Kabbalah. Kabbalah is a thirteenth-century Spanish system of theosophy that explains the inner workings of the divine psyche and the significance of human action. Professor Moshe Idel of the Hebrew University, one of this generation's great scholars of Kabbalah, has suggested that it is a doctrine built around (1) the dynamic structure of God as envisioned through the *Ayn Sof* and the *sefirot* (which we shall discuss below) and (2) its dynamic relationship with human beings through the performance of sacred deeds.

20. The inverted tree

שורש האילן

Shoresh ha-ilan

God's Tree

Sefer Ha-Bahir

Sefer Ha-Bahir was first published in Provence in 1176 but attributed by the pious to Rabbi Nehunia ben Hakana, a first-century talmudic sage. Until the *Zohar* appeared near the end of the thirteenth century, it was probably the most important kabbalistic work. The *Bahir* (which means "illumination" or "radiance") speaks about creation, the alphabet, God's emanations, and the soul. Its language is dense and often opaque. It brought together much of the work of earlier mystics and served as a touchstone for subsequent speculation.

In the following well-known passage, we are offered the image of a cosmic (inverted?) tree and, with it, the notion that all being may literally be a single organism.

> And all acknowledge that they were not created on the first day; that they should not say: [The angel] Michael stretches out the heavens in the south and [the angel] Gabriel the north while the Holy One [only] measures the middle.
>
> But I am God, the One who makes everything, I alone stretch the heavens and, unaided, extend the earth before Me. "Unaided" can also be read: "Who was with Me?" (Isaiah 44:24).
>
> I am the One who planted this tree for the whole world to enjoy. I have spread out everything within it. And I proclaimed its name: Everything. For everything depends on it

and everything issues from it; everything needs it; to it they gaze and for it they wait and from there the souls blossom in joy.

I was alone when I made it and no angel can rise above it, saying, "I came before You." Furthermore, I spread forth My earth in which I planted and rooted this tree. And I exulted alone and I exulted with them.

Who was there with Me to whom I might have revealed this secret of Mine? (1:22)

21. *Sefirot*

ספירות

Sefirot

Letters and Numbers

Sefer Ha-Yetzirah

Of all Kabbalistic images, the *sefirot* (literally, "numbers") are probably the most well known and least understood. Numbers have always held high fascination for mystics. By their very nature, they seem to hint at some hidden, inner structure of reality. With the emergence of Kabbalah in the thirteenth century, however, the "numbers" discussed in earlier varieties of Jewish mysticism now come to be understood as manifestations or emanations of God's creative process. They are frequently portrayed as ten concentric circles or "spheres" (but this has no linguistic relation to the Hebrew *sefirah*, which only means "number").

Kabbalists teach that the *sefirot* are the closest we can come to comprehending the inner workings, the psyche, of the Godhead. They are adamant that the entire sefirotic system is, in reality, a unified whole—a single manifestation of the Divine. They employ such metaphors as "the way a flame is joined to a burning coal" to help us understand how the *sefirot* "emanate" from God. Simply by being—without any intention to cause, to affect, or to create—God brings the world into being. The *sefirot* are ten orders of God's gradually diminishing presence, the last of which is our world.

The *sefirot* can also be understood psychologically. We each have tendencies, for instance, that vary between strictness and lenience. At any given time these tendencies could be said to be in or out of balance. We also have different ways of arriving at knowledge; we might have an intuition or we might have an insight. The latter connotes piercing the darkness of ignorance with a shaft of light, whereas the former seems to be mysteriously brought forth from within. And, of course, we are all aware that we have both feminine and masculine—yin and yang—sides to our personalities. A personality with only one side or the other would be not only out of balance and destabilized but literally unable to function. The ideal is to balance all such internal, psychic forces. In the same way, Kabbalists imagine that what is wrong with the world—which is itself a manifestation of the Divine—is that God's psyche, as it were, has become destabilized.

The way the world is continuously brought forth into being from God is simply out of balance, discordant. For example, at times there seems to be too much leniency or too much strict justice in the world. We ourselves, as children of the universe, also mirror this asymmetry. The goal of religious action is the restoration of harmony—within ourselves, within our world, and, ultimately, also within God.

One final image: The ten *sefirot* are also envisioned by Kabbalists as a macro-human archetype, a transitional figure between the infinite, unknowable *Ayn Sof* and our present world. This cosmic, universal human form is called *Adam Qadmon,* the primordial Adam (see section 37). In this way, each *sefirah* is literally at work both on the macro level and within every human being.

Our first text on *sefirot* comes from a prekabbalistic work, *Sefer Ha-Yetzirah,* written in the first or second century. Its title probably means something like "The Book of How Things are Formed." It is one of the earliest mystical texts we possess and it already expresses a mystic fascination with numbers. Furthermore, as we shall see in the selection below, the ten utterances of Sinai—mentions of "And God spoke" in Genesis 1, and emanations, or *sefirot*—are added to the twenty-two letters of the Hebrew alphabet (the building blocks of creation), yielding thirty-two "instruments of wisdom." In most classical diagrams, each of the ten *sefirot* is illustrated as being joined to the others through twenty-two paths or channels.

> With thirty-two awesome instruments of wisdom *Yah*, the Lord of Hosts, God of Israel, Living God and Eternal King, *El Shaddai,* compassionate and gracious, high and exalted, dwelling on high, holy is His Name, engraved. And He created His world with three principles: boundary, letter, and number. (1:1)
>
> Ten ineffable numbers and twenty-two letters are the foundation. Three mothers, seven doubles, and twelve simples. (1:2)

Figure 1 (see p. 77) shows how the ten *sefirot* are traditionally arrayed in their diagram. Above (or within or around) everything, of course, is *Ayn Sof*, the Infinite One of All Being. Creation "begins" with the top three *sefirot*, or the "head." The first is *Keter*, the crown. The second and third, *Chokhmah* and *Binah*, are modes of knowing. The fourth and fifth, *Chesed* and *Gevurah*, are the arms but also represent dimensions of parenting—both of which are indispensable in the formation of a healthy child. The sixth, *Tiferet,* is in the center; it is the torso and functions as harmonizer and is therefore also associated with beauty. The seventh and eighth, *Netzach* and *Hod,* are the organs of sexuality. Everything is balanced, like a circus act, on the top of the ninth, *Yesod*, the foundation, which is also called *Tsaddik*, a righteous person. Think of it: all of being, borne by one good person! Finally, at the bottom, the tenth, we arrive at *Malkhut*: our world; the community of Israel; the *Shekhinah* or the feminine, indwelling presence of God.

The left *sefirot, Binah, Gevurah,* and *Hod,* are feminine, as is *Malkhut*. The right sefirot, *Chokhmah, Chesed*, and *Netzach,* are masculine, as is *Yesod*. One curious surprise is that, contrary to Western sex-role stereotypes, *Gevurah*—rigor and stern judgment—is seen as feminine and maternal, whereas love and mercy are portrayed as masculine. Professor Daniel Matt once wryly suggested to me that this may have been because the author of the *Zohar* had a very interesting mother.

This sefirotic system is the heart of the *Zohar* and all subsequent Kabbalah. Not only do the *sefirot* correspond to parts of the human body and the psyche, but since they represent the core structure of being itself they are present everywhere. For Kabbalists, each *sefirah* is represented by a character in the Hebrew Bible. All the stories of the Bible are also about happenings *within* the sefirotic realm. Each color in the spectrum even has a sefirotic counterpart. The result of all this, as Professor Arthur Green of Brandeis University has suggested, is that, with the *sefirot*, the Kabbalists have effectively created a new language. Here then is the sefirotic diagram.

[Figure 1]

אֵין סוֹף

Ayn Sof
The One without End
Utterly Unknowable; Source of All Being

כֶּתֶר / אַיִן

1. Keter/Ayin
Crown, Nothingness

בִּינָה

3. Binah
Intuition, Understanding, Womb

חָכְמָה

2. Chokhmah
Insight, Wisdom, Beginning Point

גְּבוּרָה / דִּין

4. Gevurah, Din
Power, Rigor; Stern Judgment

חֶסֶד

5. Chesed
Love, Mercy

תִּפְאֶרֶת

6. Tiferet
Balance, Harmony, Beauty

הוֹד

8. Hod
Majesty

נֵצַח

7. Netzach
Endurance

יְסוֹד / צַדִּיק

9. Yesod, Tsaddik
Foundation, Righteous One

שְׁכִינָה

10. Shekhinah
God's Feminine Presence

מַלְכוּת / כְּנֶסֶת יִשְׂרָאֵל

Malkhut Kenesset Yisrael
Kingdom; Community of Israel; Apple Orchard

Petach Eliyahu *(Elijah began [to speak])*
Tikkunei ha-Zohar 17a–b

The following passage (named, as is most Hebrew literature, by its first few words) is *Petach Eliyahu*, "Elijah began [to speak]." It appears in *Tikkunei ha-Zohar*—literally, "corrections" of the *Zohar*. Though written after the *Zohar*, it has effectively been incorporated into it. This passage is one of the most famous descriptions of the sefirotic system. It was commonly included in prayer books as a meditation. Perhaps because of his ascension to heaven or his experience at Sinai paralleling that of Moses (1 Kings 19), Elijah the prophet became a particular favorite of Jewish mystics. Here he instructs a group of rabbis.

> Elijah opened his teaching this way: O Runner of Worlds, You are One but this oneness is not a number. You are beyond everything, hidden within all secrets, utterly incomprehensible!
>
> From You flow forth ten emanations, called by us the ten *sefirot*. Through them you guide both latent, secret worlds and those that are manifest. You are concealed from human beings in all of them. Even as You are within them, so do You fuse and unite them all. And woe to anyone who would try to separate out one from this cluster of ten, for that would be like trying to divide You!
>
> These ten *sefirot* flow forth in their order: one long, one short, one in between. And You are the One who guides them all. But no one guides You; no one is above You, no one is below You, nor on any side. You have appointed garments for them from which blossom the souls of human beings. And many physical manifestations you have arranged for them; they are called bodies but only in contrast to the garments that cover them.

And this is the sequence of their names: Masculine loving *(Chesed)* is the right arm. Feminine power *(Gevurah)* is the left. And the beauty of harmony *(Tiferet)* is the body's trunk in the center. Enduring to victory *(Netzach)* and glory's grandeur *(Hod)* are the two legs. The end of the body *(Yesod)* is the sign of the holy covenant on the male organ, and the holy community *(Malkhut)* is, likewise, the opening that we call the oral Torah, the teaching of the mouth. Insight-knowing *(Chokhmah)* is the inner thought process of the brain; intuition-knowing *(Binah)* is the heart of understanding. Concerning these two, Deuteronomy 29:28 says: "The concealed things belong to the Lord our God." Finally, the Crown on the top *(Keter)* is the royal crown itself; concerning her, Isaiah 46:10 says, "Foretelling the end from the beginning." It is the skull wearing *tefillin,* within which are the letters of the ineffable Name of God: *Yod hey vav hey.*

And just this is the way of the emanation of all being. It is the life force of the cosmic tree with its boughs and branches and, in the flow of that life force, it flourishes. Runner of Worlds, You are the Cause of all causes, the Reason for all reasons, You irrigate that cosmic tree with its life force, and that flowing is like a soul and life to the body. You have neither likeness nor image of anything outside or within. You created the heavens and the earth. You bring forth from them sun, moon, stars, and constellations. And on the earth, trees and grasses, the Garden of Eden; animals and birds, fish and human beings. All in order to recognize in them what is beyond and to comprehend how, through them, You guide what is above and what is below and how what is above and what is below becomes known. For no one knows You at all.

Except for You, above and below, there is no one else. You are known as Lord over everything. Each one of the *sefirot* is known by a name. And by these names angels are also called. But You have no Name that we can know, for You are beyond all their names even as You complete every name. Withdraw You from them, and every name collapses like a body without a soul.

You are wise but not with any wisdom we can comprehend. You have understanding but not with any understanding we possess. No one knows Your place; it is only to make your power and might known to human beings, to give them some vision of how You conduct your world through justice and love. For there is justice and righteousness even according to the deeds of human beings.

Law is *Gevurah,* justice is the column in the middle, righteousness the holy kingdom. Scales of righteousness are the two true foundations. An honest measure is the sign of the covenant. It is all to demonstrate how You guide creation. Nevertheless, Your justice is beyond our understanding, Your righteousness beyond our knowing; likewise, Your love beyond any attributes we might ever comprehend.

22. The worlds of separation and unity

עולם הפרוד ועולם היחוד
Olam ha-payrud ve-olam ha-yichud

The Color of Water

Moshe Cordovero, *Pardes Rimonim*[1]

We turn now to a consideration of how the One and perfect God can create and interact with the multiplicity of the world before us without compromising God's unity or perfection. As we have already suggested, the *sefirot* serve as a kind of bridge between God and the world. One famous solution is offered in the sixteenth-century work of Moses Cordovero, *Pardes Rimonim* ("Orchard of Pomegranates"). Cordovero (1522–1570) was one of the preeminent kabbalists in Safed prior to Isaac Luria.

> The One who emanates does not change, nor are there any parts that could justify saying that we can subdivide God into parts, even the parts of the ten *sefirot*. The divine reality tolerates neither change nor division except in the *outward* appearances of the *sefirot*. This can be grasped by the following metaphor. Imagine that pure water is poured into different glass bottles of varying colors, one white, one red, still another green, and so on for all ten. Once the water has been poured into each vessel it appears as if it had changed its color to that of its container. But indeed, the water has not changed at all, only its outward appearance is now different. And so it is with the *sefirot*; they are only vessels that have been prepared to receive [the divine flow], each with its own "color," according to its respective function. But the actual light itself remains without any color whatsoever. (17b, col. 2)

23. *Ayn Sof* withdrew itself
צמצם את עצמו
Tsimtsem et atsmo

The Space Within
Chaim Vital, *Eitz Chayim, Shaar Egolim v'Yosher*[2]

Another dimension of the same problem of creation is this: If God is everywhere, then how could there be room in which to make the universe? One of the most creative solutions stems from a sixteenth-century formulation of Kabbalah by Isaac Luria of

Safed (see section 38). We know most of what we know of the master's teaching from the voluminous writings of Luria's principal disciple, Chaim Vital (1542–1620).

Luria himself wrote little or nothing. His disciples signed a pledge to study their teacher's theory only from Chaim Vital. They took an oath not to induce Vital to reveal more than he wished and to keep the mysteries secret from others. However, when Vital fell seriously ill, some of the disciples bribed his brother to allow them to copy six hundred pages of Vital's writings, which they subsequently published. Vital's most well-known and comprehensive work is *Eitz Chayim* ("Tree of Life," punning on his first name). Present editions are disorganized, resulting apparently from several renditions and adaptations. In the following passage, Vital explains Luria's teaching about God's voluntary self-withdrawal or *tsimtsum*.

> Know that before emanations began or anything was even created there was a supernal light flooding all being. And this light is called *Ayn Sof,* the One Without End. It was simply everywhere. There was no empty space. You might think of it as thin air or ether. Yet from this simple light of *Ayn Sof,* all being issues. It has neither beginning nor end. Everything was this one, simple light resembling all.
>
> Then the simple thought arose to create all the worlds and begin the emanations, in order to bring to light the fulfillment of God's works and Names and designations, and this thought was the reason for the creation of everything.
>
> Whereupon the *Ayn Sof* contracted itself, leaving only a point within the center of the actual light. But the light was [also] withdrawn toward the edges that surrounded the central space. What now remained was an empty ether, void of everything, extending from the point in the center [to the edges].

This contraction was distributed equally around that empty central point in such a way that that emptiness was completely circular. There were neither corners nor angles. The *Ayn Sof* contracted itself so that it was a perfect circle. This is because the light of the *Ayn Sof* needed to be perfectly circular, and this required that this self-contraction not be more on one side than on another but be equidistant from it.

As we know from geometry, there is no form more perfect than a circle. But this is not the case with the form of a square, which has protruding angles, or with a triangle and other similar forms. Therefore the self-contraction of the *Ayn Sof* necessarily had to be a perfect circle.

There is another reason that has to do with the emanations that in the future were intended for that empty space, as we have recounted above. The idea is that the emanations would be in the form of circles. In that way all would be equally close to and joined with *Ayn Sof* surrounding them all equally. And they could receive the overflowing light of *Ayn Sof* equally from every direction. [Again,] this would not be the case were the emanations square or triangular or the like, since they have irregular, protruding corners, which would mean that some parts would be closer than others and would then be unable to receive the light of *Ayn Sof* equally at the same time....

The matter of this self-contraction was to reveal the root of judgment in order to give the principle of judgment to the worlds [being created], and that power is called the "spark of Kardinota," like the "wheat of Kardinota."

And thus, after the self-contraction mentioned above, there then remained an empty space, an ether void in the middle of the light of *Ayn Sof*. Now, at last, there was a place able to receive the emanations, the creations, the formations, and the doings *[Atzilut, Beriyah, Yetzirah,* and

Asiyah], which could draw down the light of *Ayn Sof,* a single, straight line of light. (22, col. a)

24. I have created, I have formed, I have even made. —Isaiah 43:7

כל הנקרא בשמי ולכבודי בראתיו יצרתיו
אף־עשיתיו

Kol ha-nikra vishmi ve-likhvodi berativ yetzartiv af asitiv

The Four Worlds

Shaul Boiman, *Miftachei Chokhmat Emet* [3]

Mystics of all religious traditions routinely speak of higher orders of consciousness or awareness. Charting inner (and higher) psychic space is obviously highly subjective. Yet four levels of awareness, rungs of being, reappear again and again. On the simplest level we have all had an "Ah-ha!" experience when suddenly we saw how things fit together, which until a moment ago might as well have been in another world. It is as if we were to set down the book we are reading and stand up on our chairs. Now we see the room from a new and higher vantage point. We can discern relationships and connections and systems of meaning that previously were invisible.

Jewish mystics imagine these orders of awareness as the emanative sequence through which God created the world. Using the metaphor of artistic creation, the first, *Atzilut,* is the beginning of emanation, the pure idea itself without yet even any form whatsoever. Then comes *Beriyah,* the act of creation, the initial sketch or artistic vision. Following this is *Yetzirah,* the formation, the blueprint, the musical score, the detailed instructions. Finally there is *Asiyah,* the actual work, the painting, the performance of the symphony, the building itself. Tradition finds a hint of the last three in the words of the prophet Isaiah 43:7.

This passage comes from Shaul Boiman's concise introduction to Jewish mysticism.

> From *Adam Qadmon* [the primordial human archetype; see section 37] issued countless worlds. They are all included within four, secretly alluded to in Genesis 2:10, "A river issues from Eden to water the garden, and it then divides and becomes four branches." These worlds are called *Atzilut* [Emanation], *Beriyah* [Creation], *Yetzirah* [Formation], and *Asiyah* [Making]. They issued from *Adam Qadmon's* eyes, ears, nose, and mouth. *Atzilut* from the eyes, *Beriyah* from the ears, *Yetzirah* from the nose, and *Asiyah* from the mouth of *Adam Qadmon.* And for this reason, these four are called the world of sight, the world of sound, the world of aroma and the world of speech. (sec. 13)

25. Those who walk within rivers of fire

מהלכא בנהרי נורא

Mahalkha bi-neharei nura

Akiva's Journey

"Heikhalot Zutrati" [4]

Once the mystics had postulated how the divine creative process might have emanated "down" from *Ayn Sof,* the question arose: Might it possible for human beings to swim back upstream? Might a person ascend through higher and higher orders of consciousness? Or, in prekabbalistic imagery, might one directly comprehend God? While much of our knowledge is based on fragmentary texts, we now know that there was a vibrant Jewish mystical community in second- and third-century Palestine. Through meditative techniques and devotions, these seekers tried to ascend through the palaces (or

Heikhalot) of heaven, hoping ultimately to behold God. The great talmudic sage Rabbi Akiva was widely considered one of the few who made it to the top and survived unhurt (see section 28). Some of his experiences are recounted in the following midrash.

> Rabbi Akiba [Akiva] said: "In that hour when I ascended on high, I made marks at the entrances of heaven more than at the entrances of my own house, and when I came to the curtain, angels of destruction went forth to destroy me. God said to them: 'Leave this elder alone, for he is worthy to contemplate my glory.'" Rabbi Akiba said: "In that hour when I ascended to the *Merkabah* [*merkavah*, the divine throne] a heavenly voice went forth from under the throne of glory, speaking in the Aramaic language: 'Before God made heaven and earth, He established a vestibule to heaven, to go in and to go out. He established a solid name to strengthen by it the whole world. He invited Man (to this pre-established place) to enable him[:]
>
> To ascend on high, to descend below, to drive on the wheels [of the *merkavah*], to explore the world, to walk on dry ground, to contemplate the splendor, to dwell with the crown, to praise the glory, to say praise, to combine letters, to say names, to behold what is on high, and to behold what is below, to know the meaning of the living and to see the vision of the dead, to walk in rivers of fire, and to know the lightning.
>
> And who can explain and who can behold what is before all this. It is said: For man shall not see Me and live (Exodus 33:20); and secondly it is said: That God speaks to man and he lives (Deuteronomy 5:21); and thirdly it is said: I saw the Lord sitting upon a Throne, etc. (Isaiah 6:1).'" (77–78)

6

Consciousness

We have considered how the sefirotic organism, as a diagram of the infrastructure of Being, can represent both the human form and psyche and how people can ascend through higher and higher levels of awareness. We turn now to awareness itself. The twentieth-century German philosopher Ernst Cassirer (1874–1945) once observed that all creation stories begin with light because light is a metaphor for human consciousness rising from the dark waters of unconsciousness. Throughout all world cultures, light means awareness and knowing. Let us begin literally at The Beginning, the opening verses of Genesis.

26. Hidden light

אור גנוז
Or ganuz

The Light of Consciousness
Zohar I:31b–32a; II:148b–149a

If God created the sun and moon and stars, which are all the sources of light, on the fourth day of creation, then where did the light that God created on the first day come from? The *Zohar* offers a daring solution. It suggests that the first light of creation was not optical but spiritual, the light of awareness, a light so dazzling that in it Adam and Eve were able to see from one end of space to the other end of time. (I am grateful to Professor Daniel Matt for juxtaposing these two passages in his work.)

"And God said, 'Let there be light!' And there was light" (Genesis 1:3). This is the light that the Holy One created at first. And it is also the light of the eye. And it is the same light that the Holy One showed to the primordial Adam. In it he could see from one end of space to the other end of time! And it is the same light that the Holy One showed King David, who sang God's praise, "How great is Your goodness, which You have hidden away for those who revere You!" (Psalm 31:20). It is the light that the Holy One showed Moses, in which he was able to see from Gilead to Dan.

But then the Holy One foresaw that three wicked generations would arise, the generation of Enosh, the generation of the flood, and the generation of the tower of Babel. So, in order to keep them from using it, God hid the light.

The Holy One gave it to Moses, who used it for the three remaining months he was in his mother's womb. As we read, "She concealed him for three months" (Exodus 2:2). When they were done, he came before Pharaoh. But the Holy One took it from him until he stood at Mount Sinai to receive the Torah. Then God returned the light to him and he used it for the rest of his life. And that is why the children of Israel were unable to approach him until he put a veil over his face. As it is written, "And they were afraid to come near him" (Exodus 34:30). He wrapped himself in it like a *tallit,* as it is written, "Wrapped in a garment of light" (Psalm 104:2).

"Let there be light! And there was light." Whenever the text says, "and there was," it means that it is both in this world and in the world to come.

Rabbi Isaac said that the light that the Holy One created during the work of creation shone from one end of space to the other end of time and then it was hidden away. And why was it hidden? So that the wicked of the world would not be able to benefit from it nor could worlds be despoiled through them. It is treasured away for the righteous, yes, for a righteous person! [32a] As it is written, "Light is sown for the righteous and gladness for the upright in heart" (Psalm 97:11). Then will worlds be fragrant and it will all be One. But until the day when the world to come arrives, the light is treasured and hidden away....

If the light of the first day of creation, that light of ultimate awareness, in other words, were to fall into the hands of the wicked, they would use it to destroy the world. It's true. (If we ourselves could see into the future, we'd make a terrible mess of things!) Yet if God were to withdraw the light from creation entirely, deprive it of even the possibility of ultimate awareness, the universe would collapse, implode. So how did the Holy One solve the problem? God hid the light, but only for the righteous in the time to come.

[II: 148b] Rabbi Judah said, "Were it not completely hidden, [149a] the world could not endure for even one moment! For this reason the light is hidden and sown like a seed, responsible for births and seeds and fruit. Through it, the world endures. Indeed, every single day a ray issues from that hidden light and sustains the entire world, for through it the Holy One nourishes creation.

And every place where they study Torah in the night, one thread-thin ray issues from that hidden light and flows down upon those who labor. As it is written, "By day God directs His love, at night, His song is with me" (Psalm 42:9), as has already been explained. And, as we read about the day that God's tabernacle was established below, "And Moses was unable to enter the Tent of Meeting, because the cloud was upon it" (Exodus 40:35). What is the "cloud"? It is one thread-thin ray issuing from a dimension of that primordial light, shining forth with the joy of the bride (*Shekhinah*) as it entered into the tabernacle below. And from that day on, the light has not been revealed except when it serves its purpose in the world. And in this way, every day the light renews the work of creation.

The Place of Light

Sefer Ha-Bahir

Drawing on a nuance in the Genesis account, the *Bahir* also suggests that this primordial awareness preceded creation. Consciousness thus comes before everything.

> Rabbi Berekhiah said: Why is it written (Genesis 1:3) "And God said: 'Let there be light' and there was light," instead of "'Let there be light' and light came into being"? This is like a king who had something beautiful and precious; he set it aside until he could designate a proper place where he could put it. Thus it is written: "Let there be light [but of course] there was light," for it was already there. (25)

27. The business with Ezekiel's chariot

מעשה מרכבה
Ma'aseh merkavah

Magical Mystery Tour

Ezekiel 1:1–28

Ezekiel's psychedelic vision of God's chariot is the paradigm Jewish mystical experience. Even though most of its imagery now seems hopelessly lost in antiquity, this vision of God, borne on a chariot (or *merkavah*) and carried by four creatures, has remained central to Jewish mysticism throughout history. Simply put, if you are a Jew and you have a mystical experience, you will behold the *merkavah*. So potent an image, the business with the chariot (*ma'aseh merkavah*), as we shall see in the next section, was a forbidden topic for public discussion. It may just also be the closest that biblical Judaism comes to imaging God.

We know that in the first centuries C.E. Ezekiel's vision of the chariot spawned whole communities, *yordei merkavah* ("descenders of the chariot"), seeking similar epiphanies. Much of the Hebrew describing Ezekiel's vision remains opaque and even the best translations leave us frustrated. Scholars agree that Ezekiel was a priest of the Temple before it was destroyed. The scene is Babylonia during the exile, and God, now for the first time, is revealed *outside* the land of Israel—no longer stationary on a throne in Jerusalem but literally, like the people themselves, in motion. The vision evokes the cherubim of the wilderness tabernacle in Exodus (25:18–20; 37:7–9), the glowing coals of Isaiah's throne room vision in chapter 6, and the theophanies of Exodus 20 and 24. This passage is read in the synagogue as the *haftarah* on first day of Shavuot, which celebrates the giving of the Torah.

> And it came to pass in the thirtieth year, on the fifth day of the fourth month, as I was among the exiles by the River Chebar, the heavens opened and I saw a vision of God. On the fifth day of the month—it was the fifth year of the exile of King Jehoiachin—the word of the Lord came to Ezekiel the priest, son of Buzi, by the River Chebar in the land of the Chaldeans. And the power of God was upon him there.
>
> And I looked, and behold, a thunderhead came sweeping out of the north—a great cloud and a flashing fire and surrounded by radiance. And in the center of it, in the middle of

the fire, a gleaming, like the color of amber. In the middle of it were also the figures of four creatures. And this was their appearance: they had the likeness of human beings. But each one had four faces, and each one had four wings. And their feet were straight feet; and the soles of their feet were like the sole of a calf's foot; and they sparkled like the color of burnished bronze. They had human hands under their wings; and the four of them had their faces and their wings on four sides. Their wings were joined to one another; so that they did not turn when they moved; each could move in the direction of any of its faces.

Each of them had a human face [in front], the face of a lion on the right; the face of an ox on the left; and the face of an eagle [at the back]. Thus were their faces. Their wings were stretched upward; each had two touching the others while the other two covered their bodies. And each could move in the direction of any of its faces; wherever the spirit moved them, they went.

Such then was the appearance of the creatures. With them was something that looked like burning coals of fire and torches flashing up and down among them. The fire was bright and lightning shot out from it. The creatures ran and returned like the appearance of flashes of lightning.

As I gazed on the creatures, I saw one wheel on the ground next to each of the four-faced creatures. As for the appearance and structure of the wheels, they gleamed like beryl. All four had the same form; the appearance and structure of each was as of two wheels cutting through each other. And when they moved, each could move in the direction of any of its four quarters; they did not veer when they moved. Their rims were tall and frightening, for the rims of all four were covered all over with eyes. And when the creatures moved forward, the wheels moved at their sides; and when the creatures were borne above the earth, the wheels were borne, too. Wherever the spirit impelled them to go, they went—wherever the spirit impelled them—and the wheels were borne alongside them; for the spirit of the creatures was in the wheels. When those moved, these moved; and when those stood still, these stood still; and when those were borne above the earth, the wheels were borne alongside them—for the spirit of the creatures was in the wheels.

Above the heads of the creatures was a form: an expanse, with an awe-inspiring gleam as of crystal, was spread out above their heads. Under the expanse, each had one pair of wings extended toward those of the others; and each had another pair covering its body. When they moved, I could hear the sound of their wings like the sound of mighty waters, like the sound of the Almighty, the tumult like the din of an army. When they stood still, they would let their wings droop. From above the expanse over their heads came a sound. When they stood still, they would let their wings droop.

Above the expanse over their heads was the semblance of a throne, in appearance like sapphire; and on top, upon this semblance of a throne, there was the semblance of a human form. From what appeared from his loins up, I saw a gleam as of amber—what looked like a fire encased in a frame; and from what appeared from his loins down, I saw what looked like fire. There was a radiance all about him. Like the appearance of the bow that shines in the clouds on a day of rain, such was the appearance of the surrounding radiance. That was the appearance of the semblance of the presence of God. When I beheld it, I flung myself down on my face. And I heard the voice of someone speaking.

28. The four who entered the orchard

ארבע שנכנסו לפרדס

Arba'ah she-nikhnasu le-pardes

Orchard of Awareness

Talmud, *Chagigah* 11b, 13b, 14b–15a

Probably the most famous account of the search for heightened mystical consciousness is known as the "Four Who Entered
the Orchard," recounted in several places but most fully in the talmudic tractate *Chagigah*. *PaRDeS,* the Hebrew word for
"orchard," also serves as an acronym for the four layers of meaning latent within each word of the biblical text: *peh* for *peshat,* the
simple, superficial, obvious meaning; *resh* for *remez,* the hinted at,
associational meaning; *dalet* for *derash,* the interpreted and
expounded meaning; and *samekh* for *sod,* the secret, mystical
meaning. The ecstatic ascent here, in other words, is something
accomplished through the divinely revealed biblical text. It is the
instrument, the gateway to ultimate reality and awareness.
According to the following talmudic legend, four second-century
sages set out on the great journey, but only one, Rabbi Akiva,
returned unharmed. The warning is clear: your odds are at best
three to one!

The story begins with a discussion of which topics may be
expounded in public. Like many such accounts in all mystical
literature, the seeker is confronted with deceptive visions and
misleading angels. Each level of awareness, or palace, has gate-
keepers demanding their own passwords, "seals," or secret
names of God that will protect the aspirant. By the sixth (of the
seven) palaces it appears to the *merkavah* mystic as if "one hundred million waves pour down, and yet there is not one drop of
water there, only the splendor of the pure marble stones that
pave the palace."

MISHNAH: The subject of forbidden relations may not be expounded in the presence of three, nor the business of the creation in the presence of two, nor [the business of] the Ezekiel's chariot [Ezekiel 1, 10, and Isaiah 6] in the presence of one, unless he is a sage and understands [the implications of] his own knowledge. Anyone who contemplates [the following] four things, such a pity, better he shouldn't even have been born: What is above, what is below, what is before, what is after. And anyone who does not seek refuge in the presence of his Maker—such a pity, better he shouldn't even have been born.

GEMARA: [13b] Raba said: All that Ezekiel saw, Isaiah saw. Ezekiel is like someone from a country village who saw the king, whereas Isaiah is like someone from a big city who saw the king.

Resh Lakish said: What is the meaning of the verse, "I will sing unto the Lord, for He is highly exalted?" [Exodus 15:1]. It means a song to the One who is exalted over the exalted ones. For Mar said [alluding to the four creatures in Ezekiel's vision]: The king of wild animals is the lion; the king of cattle is the ox; the king of birds is the eagle; and human beings are exalted over them all; and the Holy One, blessed be He, is exalted over all of them, and over the whole world.

Ezekiel 1:10 says, "Each of them had a human face [at the front]; each of the four had the face of a lion on the right; each of the four had the face of an ox on the left; and each of the four had the face of an eagle [at the back]." But in Ezekiel 10:14 it is written, "Each one had four faces: One was a cherub's face, the second a human face, the third a lion's face, and the fourth an eagle's face." Here the ox is not mentioned! Resh Lakish explained that Ezekiel entreated concerning it and changed it into a cherub. He said before Him: Lord of the universe, shall a prosecutor [the ox being reminiscent of the golden calf] become a witness for the defense?! [For this reason it was substituted by a cherub in the second verse.]...

[14b] Our Rabbis taught: Four men entered the orchard. And these are they: Ben Azzai, Ben Zoma, *Acher* [iterally, "other," the term used to denote Elisha ben Abuyah after his apostasy], and Rabbi Akiva. Rabbi Akiva said to them: "When you arrive at the stones of pure marble, do not say, 'Water, water!'" For Psalm 101:7 says, "One who speaks lies will not stand before My eyes." Ben Azzai looked and died. Of him Psalm 116:15 says, "Precious in the sight of God is the death of His saints." Ben Zoma looked and went mad. Of him Proverbs 25:16 says, "If you find honey, eat only as much as you need, lest you eat too much and vomit." *Acher* tore up the plants. Rabbi Akiva left in peace....

[15a]...Our Rabbis taught: Once Rabbi Joshua ben Hanania was standing on a step on the Temple Mount, and Ben Zoma saw him but did not rise up before him. So Rabbi Joshua said to him: "From where and to where, Ben Zoma?" He replied: "I was gazing between the upper and the lower waters, and there is only the width of three fingers between them, as it says in Genesis 1:2, 'And the spirit of God hovered over the face of the waters'—like a dove hovering over her young but without touching them." Thereupon Rabbi Joshua said to his disciples: "Ben Zoma is still on the outside. When was it said that 'the spirit of God hovered over the face of the waters'? On the first day of creation, but the separation happened on the second day, for Genesis 1:6 says, 'And let it divide the waters from the waters.'"

Beyond Distinctions

Dov Baer of Mezritch, *Maggid Devarav Le-Yaakov*[1]

An easier way for moderns to understand both the seductions and dangers of the mystical enterprise comes from the writings of Dov Baer of Mezritch. The Great *Maggid*, as we have already seen, uses the idea of Nothingness to describe the goal of contemplative, ecstatic prayer.

A person needs to consider himself as if he were nothing, to forget even that he exists in any way at all. Through his prayer let him become an instrument of the *Shekhinah*, the divine presence. In this way he will be able to transcend the ordinary limits of time and attain the *olam ha-machshavah,* the world of pure awareness, the highest of the ten *sefirot, Ayin,* Nothingness. In that place everything is equal: life and death; sea and dry land. Just this is the meaning of the passage in the *Zohar* II:52b: "'Why do you cry out to Me?' (Exodus 14:15) could also be read as 'How should you cry out to Me?'—that is to say, 'to Me' alludes to the highest of the ten *sefirot, Ayin,* Nothingness." But in order to attain this level of pure awareness, he must abandon himself and forget his own interests. For there it's all equal. (Indeed, it was by attaining this level that the children of Israel were able to pass unharmed through the waters of the Red Sea.) But this is not the case when a person is stuck to the phys-ical things of this world, stuck with the distinctions between good and bad, which is to say "the seven days of the building" (the seven lower *sefirot*). How can a person transcend temporality and attain an awareness of complete unity? And so it is that when a person regards himself as "something" and seeks his own needs, then God is no longer able to be clothed by him, for God is *Ayn Sof,* the

One Without End, and surely no vessel can contain Him. But, of course, this is not so when he regards himself as "Nothing." (sec. 110)

29. The other side

סתרא אחרא

Sitra achra

Seducing the Prince
Zohar II:163a

If God is both present within and the source of all being, then evil, if it is real, must also be a manifestation of God. This is not to say that God is evil, that we must accept evil, or that we are exempt from trying to repair it, only that reality seems to be divine at its core and also riddled with what must strike any reasonable observer as some very terrible things. Because mysticism is fundamentally monist, it cannot locate the source of evil in some nondivine source. Sooner or later, one way or another, everything comes from God.

In the following parable from the *Zohar* we learn that what seems evil at first might turn out to be an instrument of the Divine. That does not mean that it is not still dangerous or terrible, but that once we realize its connection with God, its power over us evaporates.

> Indeed, [even our evil inclination] performs the will of God. It's like the case of a king who had an only son whom he loved dearly. And so, on account of his love, he ordered his son to keep far away from bad women, since anyone who did so would no longer be worthy to enter the royal palace. The prince lovingly agreed to abide by the will of his father.
>
> Now it happened that outside the royal palace there was a beautiful and voluptuous harlot. After a few days the king

said, "Let me see just how devoted my son is to my request."
So he summoned the harlot and instructed her: "Go and
seduce my son so that I can test his obedience to me."

What did the harlot do? She followed the prince and
began to caress and kiss and seduce him with all her wiles.
Now if that prince turns out to be worthy and follows the
instruction of his father, he will rebuke her and reject her
and have nothing to do with her. And then his father will
rejoice in his son and bring him into the innermost chamber
of the palace; he will shower him with gifts and presents
and great honor.

And just who is responsible for all this honor bestowed
on that prince? You must say it is that harlot! Is she deserv-
ing of praise or not? Certainly praise is due her no matter
which way you look at it. Not only did she follow the instructions of the king, but furthermore she was also responsible
for all the good that befell the prince and for all the love the
king now felt for his son.

As we read in Genesis 1:31, "And behold it was *very*
good." If it had only said, "It was good," this would refer to
the angel of life, but by adding the word "very" it also
implies the angel of death, for he is certainly very good to
observe the commandments of his master.

Alien Thoughts during Prayer

Dov Baer of Mezritch, *Maggid Devarav Le-Yaakov*[2]

Another way to approach Jewish mysticism's understanding
of evil is through Hasidism's doctrine of what is called
machshavot zarot, "alien thoughts," during prayer. As we have
already seen, Hasidism frequently psychologizes theological problems. In the following example, we try to comprehend evil in the
world by first considering it as an internal phenomenon. Why,
asks Hasidism, do our wickedest thoughts assail us during our

most fervent prayers? The answer is that they are not foreign to us but dimensions of our personality that, sensing precisely this moment of holiness and healing, have come out from our psychic cellars seeking to be redeemed. Instead of futilely struggling to repress or reject them, we acknowledge that they are unfortunately also a part of ourselves. (Just as there is only one God who is the source of all being, here too there is only one person who is the source of whatever he or she thinks and does.) Only once we accept the evil as our own can we begin to heal it, ourselves, and our world.

> We read in Talmud *Shabbat* 104a that "One who comes to purify himself is given assistance from heaven." It is possible to read this as "when we see a person come to purify himself," it means he wants to pray with great devotion in the presence of God. He makes great preparation for his prayer, but when he stands in prayer he is assailed by alien thoughts. But how then shall we understand that he is helped from on high? Hasn't he already prepared himself by purifying his thoughts so that his prayer would be worthy? So how on the contrary could he receive "help from heaven"?
>
> The answer is given by our sages of old: The alien thought itself has been given to the person from the Holy One so that he can elevate it! In this way we understand the saying, "Good things are brought about by good people." Such thoughts are not accidental, but rather they have come so that we might raise them to their root in heaven— for example, a lascivious thought *[ahavah ra'ah]* or a paranoid fantasy *[yirah ra'ah]* and the like.
>
> The person pushes the evil thought away and, instead, joins himself in love to God or fear of heaven; then he will be able to complete his prayer in even greater

ecstasy, for in this way he has freed the sparks from the shards [of the alien thoughts]. Just this is the meaning of "One who comes to purify himself is given assistance from heaven."

This also explains the verse in Ecclesiastes 1:5, "The sun rises, and the sun sets—and glides [sho'ef] back to where it rises." A person rises to pray with fervor and the sun shines on him, and just a moment later the sun has set, the fervor gone. This is because an alien thought has entered his mind. And why? The second half of the verse, "and glides back to where it rises," connotes "removing, slipping out of place." As we read in *Chullin* 42b, "If the top of the femur slipped out [shaf] of its socket, the animal is *trefah*," as if to say that the Holy One arranges this for him in order that the worshipper might "glide" back to his place. The interpretation here is that the sparks go out and return to their place, to the root in holiness. And this is the meaning of "and glides back to where it rises." (sec. 167)

30. I will surely hide My face. —Deuteronomy 31:18

אנכי הסתר אסתיר פני

Anokhi haster astir panai

The Hiding Is Hidden

Siddur Baal Shem Tov, 71 [3]

Often it is not what at first seems to be evil that is the problem, but our inability to see how God is behind or within it. In Jewish mysticism this is called God hiding God's face. In the following, the Baal Shem Tov draws a lesson from the syntactical peculiarity of biblical Hebrew. To emphasize a verb, the Bible repeats the verb. The BeSHT suggests, however, that we might read the doubled verb literally, and in the following teaching suggests that there are actually two different kinds of hiding.

> "You hid your face, I was terrified" (Psalm 30:8). The Baal Shem Tov used to explain this verse by citing Deuteronomy 31:18, "*[haster asti,]* I will surely hide My face."

In order to communicate intensity of the verb idea, biblical Hebrew commonly precedes the verb with its own infinitive. English renders this double verb as "surely hide," but a close, literal reading speaks of hiding twice.

> The Baal Shem Tov said it means that the hiding is itself hidden, so that we are unable to fathom the good that is latent within the hiding. Indeed, if we could understand that some greater goodness is concealed within God's apparent absence—that the hiding is *for a reason*, then we would be able to "sweeten the harsh decree"—to discern the purpose of God's *apparent* withdrawal. The BeSHT would conclude by saying that I am more afraid of not realizing that God is hiding than I am of the actual hiddenness itself.

The first kind of hiding is tolerable. We remain convinced that even though we don't understand what's going on, even though God's face, as it were, seems concealed from us, we remain convinced of God's presence. Indeed, if we understand that God is present but only hidden—that the hiddenness, in other words, has a purpose—then our present sadness is mitigated. But when the hiddenness is itself concealed, then the terror of meaninglessness overwhelms us. Our goal, therefore, is a faith in and an abiding trust that the world is working out the way it's supposed to. And we are summoned to find the hidden meaning we trust is already there. We have a similar teaching in the name of Dov Baer of Mezritch.

Hide and Seek
Dov Baer of Mezritch, *Itturay Torah*[4]

The hiding itself can work in two ways. In this famous and charming story, Hasidic tradition captures what Abraham Heschel once called "divine anthropopathy." We routinely speak, he noted, of God as anthropomorphic, symbolically ascribing to God a human body, but we rarely consider God anthropopathically—as having humanlike feelings.

> Once Rabbi Dov Baer was walking on the street accompanied by his disciples and saw a little girl hiding in an alcove, weeping. "Why are you crying, little girl?" asked the rabbi. "I was playing hide-and-seek with my friends," replied the girl, "but they didn't come looking for me!" Rabbi Dov Baer sighed and said to his students, "In the answer and the tears of that little girl I heard the weeping of the *Shekhinah*, 'and I will surely hide My face' (Deuteronomy 31:18). I, God, have hidden Myself too, as it were, but no one comes to look for Me!" (198–199)

31. The secret wisdom of Kabbalah
סתרי חכמת הקבלה
Sitrei Chokhmat ha-Kabbalah

Hidden Wisdom
Meshullam Fiebush of Zabrash, *Yosher Divrei Emet*[5]

Sometimes, of course, what is hidden is not God's face but the very mystical wisdom we seek. Jewish mystics have long been fascinated not only with what is hidden but how the mystical enterprise itself seems unattainable. Indeed, the Hasidic master Meshullam Fiebush of Zabrash (d. c. 1795), teaches there are some things that remain secret from anyone who has not first had the prerequisite life experiences.

> There's a big difference—like the difference between night and day—between someone who meditates on God some-times and someone who meditates on God all the time. It's impossible to explain; it's really a matter of imagination.
>
> And this is what is called secret wisdom—I have heard it from my teacher, Menachem Mendl of Permishlan. *Secret* refers to something that someone is unable to communi-cate to someone else. For example, it is impossible to describe in words the taste of [a particular] food to someone who has never tasted the taste. And this is what is meant by the word *secret*. In the same way, the love or the fear of God also cannot be explained to someone who has never had the experience [of love or fear]: it is secret.
>
> How, then, can we call the hidden wisdom of Kabbalah secret? Can't anyone who wants simply open a book? And if the person can't understand it, then such a one is simply a dummy; before such a person the Talmud and the com-mentaries are all effectively secret!
>
> No, the whole idea of the secrecy of the *Zohar* or the writing of Isaac Luria is based on [the supposition that the reader has experienced] cleaving to God. For one who is worthy to experience such communion, to behold the supernal chariot [of Ezekiel's vision]; or, like the Ari, Rabbi Isaac Luria, who, through his spiritual vision continually traveled the resplendent paths of heaven; or, like the four sages who entered the mystical orchard, as has been explained in tractate *Chagigah* [see section 28]; or the commentaries of Maimonides [*Mishneh Torah, Yesoday ha-Torah,* end of chapter 4]. (22)

Part Three

*May…my heart be acceptable before You,
O God.*

—Psalm 19:15

7

Person

Jewish mysticism and ethics are inseparable; they are each expressions of our yearning to comprehend and actualize the unity of all being. If we are all manifestations of the Divine, then we are all connected to one another. This means, apart from its obvious ethical implications, that how we treat one another directly influences how the higher unity will be realized here in this world of apparent brokenness. In this way, mystical awareness leads to the desire to perfect oneself. It's just the opposite of what is commonly taught: you are not religious in order to be a better person; you must be a better person in order to be religious!

In Judaism, voluntary spiritual seclusion from the community is considered an abnormal condition. When it happens at all, it is only for the purpose of subsequently returning to the congregation with a keener sense of righteousness.

Indeed, Judaism's most influential manuals of ethical discipline have all been written by practicing mystics. The goal of awareness and the purpose of receiving Torah is to improve ourselves. The true measure of mystical attainment is measured by our communal behavior—what Martin Buber called the sphere of the interhuman. Even our most trivial acts affect worlds on high. If all being is a single organism, no act can be inconsequential, unimportant, or irrelevant.

We therefore begin Part Three with some mystical images of what and who a human being is.

32. Self

אנכי

Anokhi

God's Self Calling Yourself

Levi Yitzchak of Berditchev, *Itturay Torah*[1]

One of the core tenets of all spirituality is the paradoxical suspicion that, in the words of the late Alexander Altmann, "God is in the self, but the self is not God."[2] We sense the same divine presence both in the world around us *and* within ourselves. Naturally then, when Moses ascends Sinai and gets as close to God as any human being has ever come, we might expect an insight into our soul's relationship with God.

As Moses is sheltered in the cleft of a rock while the divine presence passes by, God proclaims, "The Lord, the Lord, is a God loving and gracious." Noting the repetition of "the Lord," Levi Yitzchak of Berditchev (see section 6) offers the following insight into our relationship with God. Just this, he says, is the reason that "Lord" is repeated: the first mentioning of "the Lord" is actually the aspect of God within Moses calling to its other, universal presence.

> "The Lord passed before him [Moses] and called out: '*Adonai, Adonai* [The Lord, the Lord] is a God loving and gracious, abounding in kindness and truth...'" (Exodus 34:6). The soul is a part, a manifestation of God on high. So, when the soul calls out to the Holy One, one part of God, as it were, is calling out to another. For this reason, when the

text says that God passed by Moses—that is, when a person is overwhelmed by the awe of the divine, filled with reverence and love—then: "[One manifestation of] God calls out" to another. (268)

33. No two human beings are alike

אין שני בני אדם שוין בעולם

Ayn shnei venei adam shavin ba-olam

A Single Gesture

Pinchas of Koretz,

Mi-Torat ha-Hasidut: Torat Rabbeinu Pinchas mi-Koretz[3]

Pinchas of Koretz (1726–1791) led a modest life, supporting himself as a schoolteacher. He once said that the *Zohar* had kept him alive and urged his followers to study it regularly. The Koretzer died on a journey to Israel. In this teaching (which was first called to my attention by Rabbi Ed Feld), Pinchas of Koretz goes beyond the classical religious notion that each human being is unique and asserts the same for every word and deed. Furthermore, since we cannot know with any certainty the implications of even our most trivial acts, the simplest word or deed performed by the least likely person might have cosmic significance.

It's possible for a person to be created and live an entire lifetime just for the sake of uttering one word or making a single gesture that he performs for the Holy One. And even if he makes a mess of everything else, who knows how he is meant to return to his divine place. Nevertheless, it was necessary that he be created for that very gesture that the world needs and that could be accomplished only through him and him alone. From the creation of the world until its end, no two people have ever been the same or ever will be. (6)

34. Returning to your source

תשובה
Teshuvah

Teshuvah *as Ultimate Reality*

Adin Steinsaltz, *The Thirteen Petalled Rose*[4]

The author of the following passage is the celebrated contemporary Israeli talmudic scholar and mystic Adin Steinsaltz. Except for Elie Wiesel, no one on the present Jewish landscape enjoys more universal acceptance or respect. Steinsaltz is prolific and is blessed with the ability to speak to scholars and laypeople alike. The source of this text is a primer on Jewish spirituality, *The Thirteen Petalled Rose*—an allusion to the lowest of the *sefirot*.

Teshuvah is usually translated as "repentance," but in the Jewish mystical tradition it is far more. As the following selection demonstrates, it is a primary religious gesture; some would argue *the* primary religious gesture. Apology and regret are only an initial and superficial manifestation. Ultimately, *teshuvah* is nothing less than a willingness to die and become one again with one's Creator. It is clicking on the computer software button that says, "Restore default configuration." It is the mother of all sacred deeds. *Teshuvah* may just finally be all God ever says: "Return to Me."

> Repentance is one of the ultimate spiritual realities at the core of Jewish faith…. Certain sages go so far as to include repentance among the entities created before the world itself. The implication of this remarkable statement is that repentance is a universal, primordial phenomenon; in such a context it has two meanings. One is that it is embedded in the root structure of the world; the other, that before man was created, he was given the possibility of changing the course of his life. In this latter sense repentance is the highest expression of man's capacity to choose freely—it is a

manifestation of the divine in man. Man can extricate himself from the binding web of his life, from the chain of causality that otherwise compels him to follow a path of no return....

Repentance does not bring a sense of serenity or of completion but stimulates a reaching out in further effort. Indeed, the power and the potential of repentance lie in increased incentive and enhanced capacity to follow the path even farther.... In this manner the conditions are created in which repentance is no longer an isolated act but has become a permanent possibility, a constant process of going toward....

The highest level of repentance, however, lies beyond the correction of sinful deeds and the creation of independent, new patterns that counterweigh past sins and injuries; it is reached when the change and the correction penetrate the very essence of the sins once committed and, as the sages say, create the condition in which a man's transgressions become his merits....

The penitent thus does more than return to his proper place. He performs an act of amendment of cosmic significance; he restores the sparks of holiness which had been captured by the powers of evil. (125–126, 132, 135, 136)

35. Descent for the sake of ascent

ירידה לצורך עליה

Yeridah le-tsorekh aliyah

Life of Piety

Dov Baer of Mezritch, *Likkutim Yekarim*[5]

We have already encountered Dov Baer of Mezritch several times. Here we have an example of a common format for popularizing ethical ideas, the numbered list. Note how the following selections, while concerned primarily with how to pray, also easily shift back and forth from epigrammatic mystical theology to sound advice on how to conduct one's life.

3. One who reads from the Torah and beholds the lights of the letters of the text, even though the person may not chant the proper melody, since the reading is done with devotion and rapture, even though the reading is incorrect, God is not so punctilious.

It's like the case of a small child, dearly loved by his father, who wants something from him. Even though he stammers and speaks incorrectly, the father still loves the little one. In the same way when a person reads from the Torah in love, since God loves him so much, God is not concerned over the technical correctness of his speech, as our rabbis have taught in Midrash *Shir Hashirim Rabbah* 2:15 [citing Song of Songs 2:4] "'And His banner *(diglo)* over me is love,' ...God says, 'His babbling *(liglugo)* is beloved to Me.'"

4. Weeping is no good; a person needs to serve God particularly in joy. Only if the tears come from the force of the joy and communion with God are they good.

6. A person needs to learn the habit of praying and singing hymns in a soft voice and even to cry out to God in just a whisper. Nevertheless, one should sing the songs and speak the words of study with all one's strength, as it is written in Psalm 35:10, "All my bones will speak." Even the cry that comes from communion with God should be in just a whisper.

9. In prayer, you need to gradually ascend from level to level, so as not to exhaust all your energy with the very first prayer. Begin deliberately, cautiously, then, in the middle of the prayers, join with God in great communion. In this way you will be able to recite the words of all the prayers with satisfaction.

Even though you are unable to commence the prayers with much devotion, you should nevertheless recite them with focus, increasing your strength little by little, until God will help you to pray with great passion.

10. You will not be able to pray properly until you experience light surrounding you from every direction; feel that light everywhere.

11. When you relinquish all your thoughts to your Creator, God will make it clear to you what you must do, as we read in Psalm 55:23, "Cast your burden on God and God will sustain you." [Even if] what you want and yearn for is a pious thing, forget about the thing and God will give you the idea you need.

14. It will happen sometimes that you will fall from your spiritual level of your own accord. [But remember,] God knows what you need. Sometimes the world causes your descent. [So remember then also:] The descent is for the sake of the ascent; [sometimes you have to go down in order to go up to an even higher level.] As we read in Psalm 48:15, "God will lead us over death," and, as we read in Genesis 12:10, "And Abram went *down* into Egypt," and then in verse 13:1, "And Abram came *up* from Egypt." "Abram" is a metaphor for the soul and "Egypt" stands for the *kelipot,* the broken shards of reality.

15. You should do your [good] deeds in secret so that it appears to others that you are not especially pious— [although] before attaining a high spiritual level, you should do your [good] deeds openly. But if this is not so, you may act openly, like the rest of the world [which is motivated by honor and reward]. Try to be pious deep inside, since even

if you're drawn after the rest of the world, as we read in Talmud tractate *Pesachim* 50b, "From doing something for an ulterior motive comes doing it for its own sake."

22a. A wise person does not make requests of the king like others who ask that their needs be satisfied. Rather, one who is wise asks only that the king [be willing to] speak with his servant and open the gates so that the servant might enter and just have a word with the king, because he knows deep inside that what he wants to say to the king is more important and worthwhile than anything else in the world. And once the king sees that he holds this more important than any other worldly pleasure or delight, then the king will love him very much.

This is the meaning of Psalm 102:1: "The prayer of a lowly man when he is faint [and pours out his plea before God]," as if to say that he postpones and restrains any mention of his own needs. He is [simply] a humble and needy person. Nevertheless he remains faint and requests nothing in particular; he only calls and pours out his heart before God, beseeching instead that God simply open all the gates of prayer. This is better to him than all the good things of the world.

36. Self-annihilation

בטול היש
Bittul ha-Yesh

Ownerless Like Torah

Yehuda Aryeh Lieb of Ger, *Sefas Emes* [6]

In section 5 we saw how Jewish mystics yearn to become one with the Divine. Such a goal first requires a loss of self. This occurs not through some glazed-over mindlessness but rather through such total absorption in and devotion to what one is doing that there is a momentary loss of one's self-awareness. The idea is to be so fully present in what you are doing that you don't have time to realize that it's you who is doing it! This is no different than what happens ordinarily during any intense experience—a romantic dinner, a breathtaking sunset, or running a race. In all these sorts of events we simply don't have time to permit a part of our consciousness the detached luxury of observing ourselves. The Hebrew phrase for such loss of self is *bittul ha-yesh*, the annihilation of selfhood—literally, "the negation of what is." This is not to be confused with humility or outwitting our natural inclination toward egotism. (Those are necessary prerequisites for being a human being.)

Bittul ha-yesh, the annihilation of selfhood, goes all the way. Once the self is out of the way, one can be more than a servant; one can be an agent, an extension, a manifestation of the divine will. Many contemporary liberals are horrified by such talk. They are convinced that this can only lead to an unthinking, fundamentalist fanaticism. We must therefore remind ourselves that (1) religious fanaticism is invariably unethical, (2) nonmystics are often fanatics, and (3) virtually all mystics have held such selflessness as an ultimate goal and nevertheless have maintained exemplary ethical lives.

The next selection is from *Sefas Emes*, Yehuda Aryeh Lieb Alter of Ger (1847–1905). We know that the Gerer rebbe was such a popular teacher that they had to build a bigger railroad station in Gura Kalwaria, or Ger, to accommodate the enormous influx of Jews who sought to hear his discourses. Professor Arthur Green of Brandeis University calls the *Sefas Emes* the crowning achievement of Polish Hasidism. It is a five-volume, enormously literate, free-associative, and profoundly spiritual collection of teachings on the weekly Torah portion. Like all of this genre, it interweaves midrashic, talmudic, and, above all, biblical allusions.

In the following text, the Gerer teaches that the real effort in learning Torah is negating one's own mind and opinion in order to understand the will of God. Only in such a way can every deed be filled with God's presence.

The whole idea for someone who strives to understand Torah is to annihilate one's own thoughts and opinions in order to comprehend what the Torah is saying and what God wants. *Midrash Bamidbar Rabbah* 19:26 likens Torah to a wilderness, which is to say that it must be ownerless like a wilderness. As it is written in Numbers 21:18, "From the wilderness to *matanah* [i.e., From the wilderness a *matanah*, or gift, has been given]." Midrash *Bamidbar Rabbah* 1:2 relates the story of a prince who entered a conquered province, whereupon all the inhabitants of one city after another fled. Then he came to a ruined city whose inhabitants [having nothing more to lose, therefore having nothing to fear] came out to greet and praise him. Whereupon the prince said, "This city pleases me more than all the others...here I will dwell."

The word *midbar,* wilderness, means to guide or to rule over. And the experience of being in the wilderness means to submit to its rule. This is to say that one must annihilate one's selfhood so that the only active power is the divine life force within him. And this is the difference between the inhabitants of the cities who fled and those who came out to greet the prince. Those who fled also feared the prince; however they still had some power of their own [unlike those who greeted the prince, who had none]. Similarly the nations of the world call God the God of gods, whereas the children of Israel are like the *midbar,* wilderness, having no power of their own whatsoever!

We speak of reverence before heaven in secret and in the open. In the open means that through knowing that God supervises everything, one is overcome with reverence. In secret means that the reverence before heaven becomes fused with one's very life force so that it is inconceivable that one might undertake any action or movement at all without remembering that it is all through the power of the Holy One; one is only an axe in the hand of the one who chops with it.

In the same way, one who occupies himself in the study of Torah has to be empty of all selfhood and be led through Torah to doing only the will and desire of the Holy One. With Torah God created the world, and through the power of the Torah one is able to cleave to the Holy One with each actual deed. Through annihilating one's self and in each deed submitting [instead] to the innermost divine life force, and through the letters of the Torah that are within every deed, we can attain the experience of doing something *lishmah,* for its own sake. Everything was created for God's glory...and the glory of God's Name.

37. A human being who contains all creation

האדם כולל בבריאתו כל הנמצאות כלם
Ha-adam kolel bivriato kol ha-nimtsa'ot kulam

Adam Qadmon

Moses Cordovero, *Pardes Rimonim*[7]

We conclude our consideration of "Person" with its consummate expression: *Adam Qadmon,* the one and ultimate human being. In section 21 we saw how the sefirotic organism can be understood as a portrayal of the divine psyche. In Lurianic Kabbalah, the *sefirot* also come to represent a primordial human archetype. Not just any individual person, *Adam Qadmon* is rather a cosmic template of the primal and ultimate human form.

However, since at its highest level all being is the divine unity, then this human archetype is a kind of halfway image between *Ayn Sof*, the unknowable, infinite unity of God, and everyday reality. *Adam Qadmon*, in other words, is itself synonymous with all the *sefirot*. Through *Adam Qadmon*, the mysterious correspondence between the divine and human is completed.

Gershom Scholem, in his *Major Trends in Jewish Mysticism*,[8] based on a series of lectures he delivered at the Jewish Institute of Religion in New York (which subsequently merged with Hebrew Union College), observed that "*Adam Qadmon* is nothing but the first configuration of the divine light which flows from the essence of *Ayn Sof* into the primeval space on the *Tsimtsum*.... He therefore is the first and highest form in which the divinity begins to manifest itself after the *Tsimtsum*. From his eyes, mouth, ears and nose, the lights of the *Sefirot* burst forth."[9]

As we have noted in section 22, Moses Cordovero was one of the leading Kabbalists of sixteenth-century Safed and the teacher of Isaac Luria. Here he writes about *Adam Qadmon*.

> Man comprises in his composition all the creatures, from the first point until the very end of [the world of] Creation, [the world of] Formation, and [the world of] Making, as it is written: "I have created him, formed him and even made him" [Isaiah 43:7]. (119)

8

Deed

As a religious tradition, Judaism is starkly behaviorist. Spiritual life is organized around a catalogue of religious deeds, or mitzvot. This is not to say that belief is unimportant or that Jews don't worry about what they do and do not believe as much as other people, but rather that Judaism understands that, while you cannot help what you believe, you are always responsible for what you do. The strategy seems to be that actions will shape beliefs and that if— God forbid—they don't, then you will at least have acted like a decent person. This primacy of deed, not surprisingly, is also reflected in all varieties of Jewish mysticism. Certainly, as we shall see in the following section, the most well-known mystical idea in the present generation likewise involves deeds.

38. Restoring the universe

תקון עולם

Tikkun olam

The Purpose of People

Chaim Vital, *Shaar haMitzvot*[1]

Isaac Luria (1534–1572)—or, as he is more commonly known, the Ari (an acronym of his initials *ha-Elohi* Rabbi Yitzchak that, in turn, means "the Lion")—promulgated a creative and daring new system of cosmology in sixteenth-century Safed that would come to be known as Lurianic Kabbalah. For the first time in Jewish thought, the creation process is described in what can only be called mythic terms.

Luria spent his youth in Egypt and moved to Safed in 1570, where he became a student of Moses Cordovero (see section 22). In the three years prior to his death during an epidemic at age 38, the Ari transformed Jewish thought. He led peripatetic classes, communed with the transmigrated souls of deceased sages, invented elaborate new devotions, or *kavanot*, to accompany the performance of commandments. Luria himself wrote nothing and forbade the propagation of his theology during his lifetime. This would have to wait for his chief disciple, Chaim Vital (see section 23).

In brief, Luria proposed that before creation God's presence filled all space. In order to make room for the world, God had to withdraw from a finite amount of space. Luria called this voluntary act of divine self-withdrawal, or self-concentration, *tsimtsum*. Into this newly created void, God then shone (or emanated) a ray of light that arranged itself into the shape of the primordial human archetype, *Adam Qadmon*—which, as we have already seen in the preceding section, is identical with the sefirotic tree itself.

This macro human contained the seed for all subsequent creation, the souls of every creature yet to be born. To contain the light, God prepared vessels, *keilim*, but at this juncture a catastrophe happened. God had underestimated the power of the light, and the lower seven of the ten vessels shattered! This cataclysm Luria called *shevirat ha-keilim*, "the breaking of the vessels." Instead of an orderly and perfect creation, the result was our present world, a heap of broken shards, or *kelipot*—each containing sparks, or *nitzotzot*, of the original divine light. (Many historians have suggested that the historic cataclysm of the expulsion of the Jewish people from Spain in 1492 influenced Luria's world-view and contributed to the popularity of his thinking.)

According to Lurianic Kabbalah, the task of human beings and the purpose of the commandments—indeed, the meaning of life—is to free the trapped sparks of light and thereby restore things to their originally intended plan, or, using Lurianic imagery, to their original root. This act of world repair and restoration is called *tikkun olam*. *Tikkun* is messianic action, wherein every deed contributes to the ultimate and sacred task of returning all things to their original place in God. Even the ineffable four-letter Name of God has been split in half by the "breaking of the vessels" and awaits *tikkun* to make it whole again.

One final frustration: *Adam Rishon* (the Adam of the Garden of Eden) could have repaired the whole thing. Had he and Eve only fulfilled the one commandment prohibiting them from eating from the tree, the entire cosmos would have been restored, history would have come to an end, and the first Adam would have become the redeemer.

> Concerning the study of Torah...[a person's] intention must be to link his soul and bind her to her supernal source by the means of Torah. And his intention must be to achieve thereby the restoration of the supernal *anthropos [Adam Qadmon]*, which is the ultimate intention of the creation of man and the goal of the commandment to study Torah.... As when studying Torah, man must intend to link his soul and to unite her and make her cleave to her source above...and he must intend thereby to perfect the supernal Tree [of Life] and holy *anthropos*. (57)

39. *Unio Mystica*

דביקות

Devekut

Communion with God

Israel Baal Shem Tov, *Tzava'at ha-Rivash*[2]

The goal for Hasidism, and perhaps for all of Jewish mysticism, is *devekut,* communion or fusion with God: to be present within the Divine. As a way of practicing Judaism, a religion of the transformative power of deed, Jewish mysticism is naturally organized around the performance of divine commandments, mitzvot, sacred deeds.

The following selections are from one of the most popular anthologies of hasidic spiritual practice, *Tzava'at ha-Rivash,* "The Testament of the Baal Shem Tov." (It was probably authored by Dov Baer of Mezritch but attributed to the BeSHT.) In this classic (1793) manual for leading a life of communion with God, we encounter a very sophisticated psychology offered in very simple terms. Indeed, it reads like a contemporary self-help book. All of its contents can be found in other anthologies of Dov Baer of Mezritch's teachings.

11. Let whatever you do not be for your own needs but for bringing pleasure to God—even if the pleasure of such service coincidentally fulfills your own needs.

12. Do not say in your heart that because you serve God with *devekut,* cleaving, that you are better than someone else. For the other person was created to serve God, and God has given the other person a mind just as God gave one to you. Why should you consider yourself superior to a worm? The worm serves its Creator with all its capacity and strength. And a human being is just another creature like even a worm or an insect, as it is written in Psalm 22:7, "But I am a worm, less

than human." Indeed, had God not given you a mind, you would only be able to serve God like a worm. This being so—that you are no different from a worm—then how much the more so with regard to other people.

Remember that you, the worm, and all the other insignificant creatures are considered as equal companions in the world. All were created and all only have the abilities they were given by God. Always keep this in mind.

34. Know that every word [in prayer] is a *shiur koma,* a whole creature, and requires all one's strength. And if one did not do so, it would be [born] lacking a limb!

40. When a person is in a place of smallness [feeling worthless], then it is better to pray from the prayer book because, from seeing the letters, one will be able to pray with *kavanah*, devotion. But when one is able to cleave to the higher world, then it is better to close one's eyes so that what one sees will not be a distraction.

42. Before prayer, bear in mind that you must be prepared to die from the intensity of your devotion. Indeed, there are those who pray with such devotion that sometimes it would be only natural for them to die after uttering only two or three words before the Holy One.

When you think this way, you will ask, what benefit or pride is there for me in this prayer inasmuch as I might die from only a single word or two? Indeed, it can only be from an act of God's great love that I even have the strength to complete this prayer and remain alive!

44. Sometimes your evil inclination can lead you astray by convincing you that you have committed a grave sin even

though it is only a mere restrictive measure or that there was no sin at all. Its intention is that you be saddened as a result and stop serving God on account of your sadness.

You must understand this deceitful trickery and respond to your evil inclination: I will pay no heed to what you say. Your only intention is to get me to stop serving God. What you say is a lie! Even if I had committed a minor sin, better I should bring pleasure to my Creator than obsessing over this infraction. You tell me about it only to get me to quit serving God. On the contrary, I will serve God in joy, for the whole idea is that my intention be not to serve myself but only to bring pleasure to the Holy One. And if this be so, then even though I do not pay attention to this minor infraction, God will not hold it against me. The principle is that I not pay attention to anything that might keep me from serving God for even one minute.

And this is a great principle in the service of God: You must avoid sadness in any way you can.

63. When you want to be in *hitbodedut,* meditative seclusion, still there should be at least one person with you, for just one person alone is in danger. There can be two people in the same room, each in meditative seclusion with God. Indeed, sometimes it happens that when you cleave to God, you are able to be in meditative seclusion even amidst a house full of people.

68. Prayer is coupling with the *Shekhinah,* the divine presence. And just as in coupling there is motion at first, so too in prayer there first needs to be swaying. Later on, one is able to stand motionless, cleaving to the divine in *devekut,* great rapture.

From the power of swaying, one is able to attain *hitorerut,* great awakening. One asks oneself, why am I making myself sway like this? This is because surely the divine presence stands before me. And from this realization one will attain *hitlahavut,* great ecstasy.

73. One should only pray in seriousness, *koved rosh,* literally, heaviness of head (*Berakhot* 30b). This means that you should not pray for something you lack, because your prayer will not be acceptable. Rather, you want to pray for the "honor of the head," because what you lack is also a lack in the *Shekhinah,* the divine presence, which is also known as the "Head." A person is a part of God on high and any deficiency in a part is a deficiency in the whole, just as the whole feels the deficiency of the part.

Therefore let your prayer be for a lack in the divine presence. Just this is the explanation of praying from the midst of heaviness of head.

75. Rabbi Israel Baal Shem commented on Genesis 6:16 [from the Noah story]: "You shall make a skylight for the *teva* ["ark" or, "word"]." This means that the words [of prayer] should radiate light. In every single Hebrew letter there are worlds and souls and divinity. These ascend and are joined and are fused to one another and to the Divine and ultimately all the letters are brought together and assembled into a word—a true unity with the Divine. A person must therefore include his or her soul in each of these dimensions. In this way one can unify all the worlds and raise them up, bringing great joy and gladness without end.

This is also the meaning of the concluding words in the verse, "[Make the ark] with bottom, second, and third decks." This is an allusion to worlds and souls and divinity. As we read in *Zohar* III:159a, "[The Holy One is concealed in] three worlds." You must listen to every word you utter because it is the *Shekhinah,* the divine presence, also known as *olam ha-dibbur,* the world of speech, who is really speaking. And, for this reason, each word has a skylight from which shines light, bringing pleasure to the Creator. All this requires great faith—indeed, the *Shekhinah* is also called an artist of faith, and without faith, God forbid! It is as the words of Proverbs 16:28, "A grumbler alienates an intimate friend."

And this is the meaning also of the words in our verse, "to within an *amah,* a cubit, of the top, you shall finish [the window, i.e., the prayer]." The word *amah,* cubit, can also be read *imah,* mother [which in sefirotic imagery can mean either *Binah,* the third *sefirah,* or *Malkhut,* the tenth].

It is also possible to read this another way: Once the word has left your mouth, there is no longer any need to remember it, since you do not see it ascend to a higher place in the same way that one is unable to look at the sun. This is the meaning of "to within a cubit of the top, you shall finish [it]." Similarly, you can achieve this in the words of Genesis 7:1, "[And God said to Noah,] Come, you and your entire household, into the ark." That is to say: Enter the word with all your body and all your strength!

130. It is reasonable to wonder why [when everywhere else in the creation account it only says, "It was good."] Genesis 1:31 specifies, "And behold, it was very good" However, in Deuteronomy 30:15 we read, "See, I have set before you life and good, death and evil." [If everything was very good, then] where did the evil come from? We cannot read this as if evil were actually real; rather, the evil is also good, except that it is on a lower level than the completely good. And this is hinted at when the *Zohar* I:49b speaks of "from above and from below."

In this way when one does good, then the evil is also transformed into good. However when committing sins (God forbid!), then the evil is made manifest. This is like the case of a household broom, designed to sweep the house. It is fairly good, even on its low level. But when it is used to strike a child who is misbehaving, then the broom is transformed into something completely evil.

Abrading Two Surfaces

Menachem Mendl of Vitebsk, *P'ri ha-Aretz*[3]

As we just saw, *devekut* means fusion with the Divine. The root meaning of the Hebrew *dalet, bet, kuf* means more than just to "cleave to"; the main idea of such cleaving to God is that there be no interposition, no barrier whatsoever between the self and God. How does one dissolve the barrier? In this Hasidic text by Menachem Mendl of Vitebsk (1730–1788), we are reminded that our inability to remain focused, our proclivity to distraction, stands between us and our goal.

> *Ve-atem ha-deveikim,* "and you shall cleave to the Lord Your God" (Deuteronomy 4:4). The whole idea of cleaving to God means that there can be no barrier, no interruption [between you and God]; only then can *devekut* happen. The Baal Shem Tov offered the following parable. It is impossible to glue two pieces of silver to one another without first scraping or scouring the two surfaces—otherwise there would be nothing to which the glue might adhere. Only then can fusion occur. Isaiah 41:7, "The carpenter encourages the blacksmith; he says of the fusion [punning on *devek* and *devekut*], 'it is good'"; thus, they are made one. In the same way, if there is rust or anything already on the surface of the metals to be joined, then it will be impossible

to glue them permanently together. And this is the meaning of the verse in Proverbs 2:4, "If you seek it as you do silver." In the same way, one who would cleave to God must also first prepare his soul so that there be no trace of rust or any other barrier that might be in the way. Only then will he, at last, be freed from grabbing onto other distractions and be able to cleave continually to God. (65)

40. For the sake of unifying God

לשם יחוד קודשא בריך הוא ושכינתיה

Le-shem yichud Kudsha Berikh Hu ush-khintei

Even at the Mall

Alexander Susskind, *Yesod ve-Shoresh ha-Avodah*[4]

Alexander Susskind ben Moses of Grodno (d. 1793) was a Lithuanian Kabbalist who led a secluded and severe religious life. His *Yesod ve-Shoresh ha-Avodah*, a very popular book of ethics and religious practice, was first published in 1782. Rebbe Nachman of Bratslav said of him that "he was a Hasid even before there was Hasidism." In this selection we are advised to bring our devotion to God into every deed we perform (*yichudim*, or "unifications") and, in so doing, bring together the "broken" letters of God's Name(s). In sefirotic imagery, the unification of *Kudsha Berikh Hu* (Aramaic for "The Holy One of Being") with *Shekhinatei* (Aramaic for "God's indwelling presence") refers to the union of the *sefirot*, *Tiferet* with *Malkhut* (section 21).

> And so it is for everything a person does, whether it be fulfilling a divine commandment or anything else one might do, say that its purpose is for the sake of unifying [*yichud*]

the Holy One of Being with the presence of God [*Kudsha Barikh Hu uShekhinatay*] and so may a person evoke the Name of the Holy One over every deed, a pervading spirit of sanctity. For without such prior focus on each deed, everything will be defiled, as is explained in the holy *Zohar, Parashat Tazria,* III:51b: "Rabbi Eleazar said that everything a person does must be for the sake of holiness. And how does one do that? One must invoke God's Name over every deed; let everything be for the service of God rather than for the *sitra achra*, the other side. Such defilement is an ever-present possibility over each deed!" And so with everything one does, if you build a new house or buy something from someone else, let it be with [this intention of] *yichud*. (637)

41. Awakening below causes awakening on high

עַל יְדֵי אִתְעָרוּתָא דִּלְתַתָּא בָּאָה אִתְעָרוּתָא
דִּלְעֵילָא

Al yedei ataruta dilatata ba'ah ataruta dele-eilah

Awakening Above from Below

Menachem Mendl Krengel,
Devash ve-chalav, in Itturay Torah[5]

In addition to the meditative *yichudim* of uniting or bringing things together that we have just discussed, we find a recurring theme in Jewish mysticism that things in this world correspond to their "roots" in a higher world. The task of humanity is to initiate the motion. As we read in the following commentary on Abraham's encounter with the angels, first we "draw near" to heaven, and this evokes a similar response from above. Menachem Mendl Krengel (1847–1930) was a Polish rabbinical commentator and biographer.

In this passage, the teaching springs from a peculiarity of biblical Hebrew syntax.

> *"Vayera eilav Adonai,* [literally:] "And there appeared to him, the Lord" (Genesis 18:1). The [commentary] *Or Ha-Chayim,* noting the Hebrew word order, asks why does the Torah put the one who sees before the One who is seen? One would expect the logical sequence to be [as the English translation customarily renders it] "And the Lord appeared to him."
>
> It is possible to say, according to Maimonides in *The Guide to the Perplexed,* that one cannot ascribe to the Holy One any change, variation, or motion. Moreover, we find in the stories of the Bible, such as the one before us, "And the Lord appeared to him" and the like, that there is no intention to remove God from God's place [of being perfectly motionless], but rather that God's drawing near or God's revelation to human beings depends on us drawing near to God and not the other way around.
>
> For example, we notice the sequence of the loving in Song of Songs 6:3, "I am my beloved's and my beloved is mine" [which implies that first I give myself to my beloved, and only then does my beloved give to me]. This is really just another way of saying that according to a person's spiritual readiness and preparation will he attain an awareness of God. [Only then] will ultimate awareness fill him with the ability to lovingly comprehend God. The same idea is also written in Proverbs 8:17, "Those who love Me, I love; and those who seek Me will find Me." [Again, note how first comes our love for God, which is only then followed by God's response.]
>
> In the language of the kabbalistic maxim, "from awakening below comes awakening on high," this explains the strange syntax of "And there appeared to him, the Lord." (120)

42. Our service fulfills a cosmic need
עבודה צורך גבוה
Avodah tsorekh gevohah

God's Chiropractor
Isaac ben Chaim of Vlozhyn, *Nefesh ha-chayim* [6]

Not only do our deeds reverberate on high; in Jewish mystical tradition they also have the capacity to actually restore the balance of the universe. Every human deed thus has potentially cosmic significance.

Isaac ben Chayim of Volozhyn (d. 1849) headed a yeshiva and maintained its operation even after the Russian government officially ordered it closed in 1824.

Today we often forget that, as with most religious revolutions, early Hasidism faced fierce opposition. In many communities, especially in the more "cerebral" Lithuanian north, the *mitnagdim*, or opponents of the Hasidim, were very powerful. We now suspect that the Volozhyner, as the respected head of a talmudic academy, may have been a crypto-Hasid, in addition to being a Kabbalist. In the same year his yeshiva was officially closed by the government, Isaac ben Chayim of Volozhyn published *Nefesh ha-chayim*. In it he developed a system of kabbalistic psychology that he hoped would lead the reader from there on to the worlds of Talmud.

> And this is what it means to be a human being: Each individual ability within a person is arranged so that it corresponds to something specific on high, something according to the secret of the *shiur koma* [God's stature; body of *Adam Qadmon*, the primordial human archetype, the sefirotic organism], which contains all the abilities and all the worlds. Everything is arranged, as it were, according to the plan of

the form of the *Adam Qadmon* (as was explained in chapter 5, section 21).

In this way, each one of the commandments is linked to and depends upon the source of its supernal root in the arrangement of the sections of the "chariot" and the *shiur koma* of all the worlds. For each individual commandment in its root includes myriad powers and lights according to the order of the *shiur koma.*

This is written in the *Zohar* (*parashat Yitro,* II:85b), "All the ordinances of the Torah are fused in the supernal King [each one with its own location]. Some originate from the head of the King, others from the body or from the hands of the King, and still others from his feet."

This matter is further explained in *Tikkunei ha-Zohar* (70:129b) and in the *Zohar* (*parashat Terumah* II:165b), "In that Name [of God] are included all 613 commandments of the Torah, and in that Name are included all the mysteries of what is above and what is below [including all of the upper masculine worlds and all of the lower feminine ones]. All those commandments are sinews and limbs through which to behold the mystery of the One of Faith. A person who does not heed and contemplate the mysteries of the commandments of the Torah does not know or comprehend how to set right the sinews and limbs of this ultimate mystery. And all the limbs of this [mystical] body are the commandments of the Torah." This is also discussed by Rabbi Isaac Luria [the Ari] in *Sha'ar ha-Yichudim.*

And in this way, when a person performs the will of the Creator, fulfilling one of the commandments through the energy within a particular bodily limb, that [act of] setting right reaches to and is received by the corresponding energy of the world on high. [Just this is the goal:] to set it right, to raise it up, to add light and [even more] holiness to the one who desires, even as it is the will of Supernal One. [This is all] according to the measure and manner of whoever performs it. And it is according to the merit and purity of his intention at the time when he performs the holy deed that is fused with the good deed itself. [This is also] according to the spiritual level of that world and its supernal power.

From there are also drawn [back] down holiness and vital energy to the power [of the limbs] of the one who performed the deed. And when one wholeheartedly does all the commandments—in all their specificity and detail [in keeping] with the core idea—he joins them to the holy power and purity of his own thought, he thereby restores the proper balance to all the upper worlds. And then all his vital energy and limbs are transformed into a *merkavah*, a chariot for those supernal, holy worlds. And the presence of God is continually upon him.

As we read in the *Zohar* (*parashat Terumah,* 155a) "'Everyone who is called by My Name, I have created him for My glory, I have formed him, I have made him' (Isaiah 43:7). 'I have created him for *My* glory,' it says! The secret of this phrase can be explained thus: The mystery of the glory that is beneath the holy throne cannot be perfected on high save through human action."

43. To sense the sacred
להרגיש הקדושה
Le-hargish ha-kedushah

Way to Go Tsaddik

Kalonymous Kalman Epstein of Cracow,
Ma'or va-Shemesh[7]

Kalonymus Kalman Epstein of Cracow (d. 1823) was a disciple of Elimelekh of Lyzhansk and Yaakov Yitzchak Hahozeh, the Seer of Lublin. Like most Hasidic rebbes of his time, he was under constant attack from establishment rabbis who ridiculed his new interpretation of Judaism and his emotional fervor during prayer. His main work, *Ma'or va-Shemesh* ("Light and Sun"), a Torah commentary, was published in 1842, almost twenty years after his death. It remains one of the fundamental works of Jewish spirituality. During a discussion on *parashat Vayetze* (Genesis 28:10–32:3), which chronicles Jacob's flight from Esau to Haran, Kalonymus Kalman wonders how the patriarch knew which way to go.

> I have heard from the wisest of my teachers, that when a holy person journeys from one place to another, then the Name of the Holy One of Being goes before him to [help him] scout out the right path.

Presumably, that's how Jacob was able to stay on course. But then Kalonymus Epstein poses a more difficult question. But what if you're not a *tsaddik* on the level of Jacob? What if you're just an ordinary Jew who wants to know which path to take? Epstein:

> If that holy person has not attained a high enough level of awareness to be able to see the Name of the Holy One of Being going before him so that in his heart he doesn't know which way to go, then let him instead him [learn to] *feel the holiness* [of one way over the other].... If you are on the way you have chosen and you don't sense an interruption of your presence within God, then you know that the way before you is the right one. If, on the other hand, you sense that you are no longer aware of your presence within the divine, then you should stop and journey no further in that direction, for the Light of the Holy One of Being does not dwell there. (77, col. 1)

In other words, does the path you are presently on make you more or less aware of the presence of God, of what you call sacred or holy? You learn to listen to and trust your own intuition, your own gut sense of how it feels. Some will argue, but what if you're a sociopath? Then you can't be guided by feelings and intuitions. And I agree, if you're psychotic, this advice might make things worse.

This may be all you'll ever have to go on. A wise man taught me once that there are people in the world who are nurturing for you. Something about who and how they are sustains, enlivens, and heals you. And there are people who are toxic for you. Something about who and how they are poisons and fragments you and makes you say and do stupid things. The name of the game, he said, is to stay far away from toxic people and close to nurturing ones. Well, it's the same with which is the right path for you: the one where you are more aware of your presence within the divine.

9

Yearning

The psalm with which we began our journey now seems so far away. Again and again in our lives and search, the distance between the initial spark of wonder at the awe of creation and the yearning to be a human being worthy to stand in God's presence seems a chasm. Indeed, the opening line of the psalm itself, "The heavens rehearse the presence of God," seems hopelessly distant from the conclusion, "May...my heart be acceptable before You, O God." And yet the beginning and the end are inextricably joined, wonder to yearning, simple awareness of the Divine to the ultimate passion to set the world right. The Jewish mystical tradition, like its parent religion, invariably returns to right acting and the vision of a time when the Holy One(ness) of all Being will be unmistakably apparent. Despite our chronic skepticism, we begin to suspect that such awareness is very close at hand and that a life of holiness is a real possibility, even for us. It is all a function of how much divine presence we can imagine. In the following texts, it is a great deal indeed.

44. It's all from the One of Blessing

הכל הוא מאתו יתברך

Hakol hu me-ito Yitbarakh

The Letter Vav *as Ego*

Menachem Mendl Morgenstern of Kotzk, *Itturay Torah*[1]

Menachem Mendl Morgenstern of Kotzk (1787–1859) is one of the most creative and tragic of all the Hasidic masters. Because he was obsessed with trying to speak the truth at all costs, those who studied in Kotzk had to be prepared to endure intense spiritual scrutiny. Reports differ, but all seem to agree that after an explosive "incident" at the Sabbath table, many disciples left for other schools and Menachem Mendl went into seclusion for the remaining twenty years of his life.

The following teaching springs from an almost preposterously close reading of two verses in the Genesis story where Abraham sends Eliezer, his servant, to get a wife for Isaac. The Kotzker notes that the word for "perhaps," *ulai*, can be correctly spelled in Hebrew as either *aleph, vav, lamed, yod* or simply *aleph, lamed, yod*—without the letter *vav*. He suggests that it may be an allusion to Eliezer's ulterior motives and ego. Like most of us, Eliezer's belief that he was running his own life blinded him from recognizing God's continuous participation and direction. Every now and then we too are blessed to realize that perhaps something else is "coming down," something much larger than our own plans and motives. Such a realization need not deprive us of our freedom but, on the contrary, enables us to recognize our destiny and ultimate place in a divine scheme we can only partially glimpse.

> And the servant said to [Abraham], "Perhaps [spelled with the Hebrew letter *vav*], the woman will not be willing to come after me to this land; shall I bring your son back to the land you came from?" (Genesis 24:5).

"And I [Eliezer, the servant] said to [Abraham], 'My master, perhaps [without the letter *vav*] the woman will not come after me.' And he said to me, 'The God before whom I have walked will send His messenger with you, and He will prosper your way.'" (Genesis 24:39-40).

Why [rhetorically asks Menachem Mendl of Kotzk], when Eliezer first asked Abraham himself the question, was the word "perhaps" *(ulai)* spelled full—that is, with the letter *vav*? Might it possibly be some kind of hint as to Eliezer's personal intention?

The explanation is that at the beginning of the story, Eliezer felt no connection with the matter. [He was a dutiful servant, but not aware that anything sacred was happening.] It is like the case of when a person is occupied in a particular matter while his heart is directed off to one side or onto some other private motive. [He is filled with his own ego.] And this blinds him from seeing his own connection [to something larger] so that he remains convinced that he is traveling in the proper direction.

Thus, only afterward did Eliezer see that this whole thing came directly from God—that Rebecca was supposed to marry Isaac all along, but his ulterior motive that Isaac marry his own daughter had corrupted his thinking. Only then did he fully realize that from the very beginning, when he first spoke to Abraham, "perhaps (spelled with a *vav*) the woman will not be willing," he had had a personal interest in the matter and was really only seeking his own welfare. For this reason, "Perhaps" is written with a *vav* at the beginning of the *parashah*, but without one at the end. (194)

A Piece of Bread

Zev Wolf of Zhitomir, *Or ha-Meir* [2]

Zev Wolf of Zhitomir (d. 1798) was a student of Dov Baer of Mezritch. His *Or ha-Meir* is a commentary on the Torah, the five scrolls and the festivals. It remains a classic. In the following teaching in the name of the Baal Shem Tov, we are offered one of the purest expressions of God's active participation in even the most seemingly trivial events—the eating of a particular piece of bread or the drinking of a particular glass of water.

Most of the time, when we speak of divine participation in the world, we assume that it is only occasional; the rest of the time God is inactive and absent, leaving us free to do as we please. Yet if, as we read below, God is involved in everything, small and great, all the time, then the very notion of God intervening collapses. God is involved in everything all the time. In such a world-view, ordinary notions of God's infrequent and miraculous intervention dissolve into a continuous divine presence. God *is* everything.

I have heard it taught with regard to Samuel of Ramah (1 Samuel 7:17): "Then he would return to Ramah, for his home was there." And I have heard that the Baal Shem Tov used to interpret Psalm 37:23, "The steps of a person are directed by God, and He delights in his way."

He said about those people who journey to faraway lands on business or for other reasons, wandering far and wide: God's plans are different from theirs. [Isaiah 55:8, "For My thoughts are not your thoughts."] They are convinced in their own minds that they are on business journeying to distant lands, wearing out their shoes, so that they can make more money. But indeed, the Holy One has something else in mind, knowing better than they how to arrange their affairs.

Sometimes, for instance, there is a particular loaf of bread for that person in some faraway land that is connected to a dimension of that person's being. And it must be eaten in precisely that place and at just that time. Or, perhaps there is a particular mouthful of water waiting to be drunk in just that place. This is the meaning of the verse, "The steps of a person are directed," wandering far and wide, hundreds of miles. And all this, the loaf of bread, the drink of a little water or something else, is in order to complete something in that person's soul.

Sometimes the whole journey does not even concern that person but one of his or her Jewish servants. Instead there might be for the servant a loaf of bread or a pitcher of water waiting in that place who might not have it in his power to make a journey to such a distant land. And just this is the real reason for the master's decision to make the trip to exactly that place. And all in order that the servant be able to consume the bread or drink the water that has been appointed for him there.

And this is the wisdom of God's decree: To complete one's soul by gathering together its scattered parts. It is how God works. And this is what is hinted at in the Psalm, "The steps of a person are directed by God," causing a person to journey to a faraway land. Everything is from God. It is all according to the wisdom of God's decree in order to complete one's soul in a way that only God understands. All the while the person has no idea. But as the rest of verse from Psalms says, "God delights in his way." Even though the person thinks he is only on a business trip, it is all from God. (214, col. 2)

45. I set the Lord before me continually.
—Psalm 16:8

שויתי ה׳ לנגדי תמיד
Shiviti Adonai le-negdi tamid

Equanimity

Israel Baal Shem Tov, *Tzava'at ha-Rivash* [3]

Carrying the idea above to its logical conclusion, we can understand one of the most illusive and central notions of the

Jewish mystical tradition. *Hishtavut,* or equanimity, is an approach to everyday life predicated on God's continuous and uninterrupted participation in everything that happens. This does not mean that you have to like what happens or that you are not allowed to try to change things, but it does mean that ordinary pleasure and pain over what one is dealt (and what one achieves) is unproductive and distracting. The psychological curve ball is that such an attitude does not lead to inaction. Indeed, believing that God is present in everything changes nothing. We wind up doing what we would have done anyway, but now we do so with greater reverence and gratitude. We are liberated from transient praise and scorn, pleasure and pain, to concentrate our full energies on being servants of God.

We have already read above (in section 39) selections from *Tzava'at ha-Rivash,* "The Testament of the Baal Shem Tov." Here we consider an elegant and straightforward expression of *hishtavut.*

2. "I have set the Lord before me continually" (Psalm 16:8). The Hebrew for "I have set before me" is *shiviti,* which is constructed from the same Hebrew root—*shin, vav, hey,* "to be equal," as the word *hishtavut,* "equanimity." This teaches that whatever happens to a person, whether it be the praise of others or their scorn, or anything else, it's all the same. And likewise with whatever one eats, whether delicacies or ordinary food, let it all be viewed as equal. And thus one's urge to evil will be removed.

Similarly, with anything that happens, let the person say, "Isn't this also from the Holy One and if it be fitting in God's eyes...." Let all one's intentions be solely for the sake of heaven, whereas one's own gain or pleasure is of no concern. Such equanimity is a very high level of awareness.

3. And so a person needs to serve God with all one's might, since everything is required by Heaven and the Holy One wants to be served through everything we do.

Sometimes, for example, a person must go on a journey or enter a conversation with others and therefore neglect the study of Torah. For this reason one needs to continually cleave to the Holy One in order to join things to their spiritual root. And so when a person goes on a journey and is unable to pray or to study Torah as usual, one needs to find other ways to serve the Holy One.

One should not be distressed by this, for God desires that we serve God in *all* ways, sometimes in one way, other times in another. And this is the reason that the journey or the conversation with others has been appointed—precisely in order to serve the Holy One in this new way.

4. Proverbs 16:3 is an important principle: "Entrust your affairs to the Lord, and your plans will succeed." Regard everything that happens as if it were appointed by the Holy One. Continually ask from God what God deems for your own good—and not what other people think. What seems like it's good in your eyes may be bad. Entrust everything, all one's concerns and needs, to the Holy One.

The Princess and the Bathhouse

Elijah de Vidas, *Reishit Chokhmah* [4]

Elijah de Vidas (d. c. 1593) lived in Safed where, along with Eleazar Azikri, author of *Yedid Nefesh* (section 14), he was a student of Moses Cordovero (section 22). He authored one of the classical works on kabbalistic ethics covering all aspects of Jewish life, *Reishit Chokhmah*. This book, and a few others like it, served to disseminate Kabbalah to a broad popular audience in the seventeenth and eighteenth centuries. De Vidas balanced the notion, popular in his time, that one should serve God only from fear, with the expectation that one should also serve God out of love.

In this passage, which begins as an almost ribald parable, we learn of equanimity and the role of sensuality. The author is careful, however, not to condemn our erotic impulses. After all, they too have a divine source. The question before us should be, what is the goal?

We have it in the writings of Rabbi Isaac of Akko that one day a princess emerged from the bathhouse and a man who was sitting there sighed a deep sigh and said, "Oh that someone would let me do with her as I please!" Whereupon the princess replied, "In the cemetery but not here!" When he heard this, he was overjoyed because he thought she meant for him to go to the graveyard and wait for her there. Then she would come to him and he could have his way with her. But this was not her intention; she meant that only there are small and great, young and old, unimportant and honored all alike (Job 3:19), but here it is not that way. It is impossible for one of the masses to even approach a princess.

So that man arose and went to the cemetery and waited there, devoting all his thoughts to her, continually imagining her form. And, from his great desire for her, he separated his thoughts from every superficial and sensual thing, concentrating instead on the form of that woman and her beauty. And so he waited, day and night, in the graveyard. There he ate and drank and slept. He thought, if she doesn't come today, she will come tomorrow. And so it went for a very long time.

He separated himself from everything sensual and continually concentrated all his thoughts on one thing. And through his concentration and his complete yearning, his soul cleaved to matters of the intellect until he had separated himself from everything sensual, even the woman her-self. And thus, casting off every sensual desire, yearning for knowledge of the Divine, he cleaved to God and became a perfect servant and a holy man. And thus his prayer was heard and his blessing was effective for all those who passed on the road. Merchants, soldiers, and people on foot who passed by would stop to receive his blessing. His reputation spread far and wide.

The teaching goes this far for our concerns. He elaborated at length on the deeds of this ascetic, and Rabbi Isaac of Akko wrote about the deeds of the ascetics that a man who does not desire a woman is like a donkey or worse. This is because from sensuality he is able to purify himself in the service of God, as we have explained. (261–262)

46. Every single utterance is an entire universe
כל דיבור ודיבור הוא עולם מלא
Kol dibbur ve-dibbur hu olam malei

Orchard of Souls

Nachman of Bratslav, *Likkutei Moharan*

Nachman of Bratslav (1772–1810), great-grandson of the Baal Shem Tov, was a literary and religious genius. We suspect now that he may also have been a manic-depressive. He believed that he was *the* righteous one of his generation. He built such a powerful bond between himself and his disciples that, when he died of tuberculosis at the age of 38, they never appointed a successor. Bratslavers today are still referred to as Hasidim of the "dead rebbe." His stories are Kafkaesque and densely symbolic. His theoretical writing is so poetic and evocative, it seems meditative.

The following selection comes from Nachman's collected teachings, *Likkutei Moharan*, "Selections from *Moreinu* (our rabbi), Rabbi Nachman." It is only the first third of the discourse. Nachman suggests that the words of our prayers are flowers woven into a bouquet for God. Within each utterance is a soul. Sometimes it seems that the author thought that he himself was "the master of the field"; other times, "the master" might be the messiah or even God.

1. Know that there is a field. And therein grow trees and plants, so lovely and beautiful. The beauty of the field and its plants is beyond words, but happy is one who has beheld it.

Those trees and plants, they are holy souls growing there. So many naked souls, always wandering outside the field, yearning to be repaired so they might be able to return to their places. Even great souls, upon which so many others depend, once they leave the field, it is difficult to return. But all the souls look to the owner of the field, for the owner is able to heal them.

One soul [for example] can only be repaired through the death of another, while another soul, only through the religious deed or service of another.

Now someone who wants to gird his loins and offer himself as the master of the field must be strong and resolute, a mighty warrior, and a sage, a truly great *tsaddik*. Such a person must indeed be extraordinary. There is one who can complete the work only with his own death. And even such a one must be extraordinary, for already there are many great ones who cannot complete the task even with their deaths. Only one who is on the highest spiritual level is able to complete the task during his lifetime. There will be so much suffering and hardship. But on account of his extraordinary mettle, he will finish the work of the field.

Once such a person is worthy to restore the souls and bring them back inside, then prayer will be especially sweet, for [only] then will the prayer itself be complete.

Just this is the owner of the field: one who is constantly watching over and trying to nourish the trees so they grow, constantly tending the field. Moving one tree just the proper distance away from another so that it does not starve out its neighbor—sometimes a very great distance is required.

2. And know that when the souls produce fruit, they are fulfilling the intention of God. Then the eyes of the owner of the field grow bright, for they are able to behold the place he must see. This is, as we read in Numbers 23:14, "the field of foresight." But when they do not perform the will of the Holy One (God forbid!) then it becomes a field of tears, as we read (*Ohalot,* chapter 18; *Moed Katan* 5b), for weeping interferes with seeing, as we read in Ecclesiastes 12:2, "And the clouds return after the rain," and our sages interpret *Shabbat* 151b, "This is the seeing, which becomes dim after tears."

But when his eyes are bright with vision, it becomes a field of visionaries. And then he is able to behold everyone, bringing them to fulfillment. This is to say, he is able to gaze on the utterance of each person and, if it is not yet complete, still distant from its goal, then he brings it to completion and then the utterance is fulfilled.

This is because each and every utterance is a whole universe, and when a person rises to pray and utters a word of prayer, then he gathers beautiful shoots and blossoms and flowers. When a person walks in the field and arranges the blossoms and flowers, one to another, until he has gathered one bunch. And so he continues adding one bunch to another until he has made a bouquet. And so he goes, gathering one beautiful cluster after another.

It's the same with prayer—only now he is collecting letters of the alphabet, assembling them into syllables, which, in turn, he fashions into whole words. Then he joins words to one another, gathering more and more until he has completed one blessing. He gathers still more, moving from the first blessing (the parents) on to the second (God's power) and the third (God's holiness) and on and on. Now who could offer fitting praise for the bouquets and garlands gathered and arranged by someone through the utterances of prayer?

Now when the utterance goes forth, it issues from the soul, as we read in Genesis 2:7, "And Adam became a living soul," as it is interpreted in Aramaic, "a speaking spirit." An utterance issues and is heard by one's ears, as our rabbis taught in *Berakhot* 13a, "Hear with your ears what comes out of your mouth." Then the utterance pleads with the soul not to leave it alone. No sooner, for example, has the letter *bet,* the first letter of *berakhah*, blessing, gone forth than it begs the soul not to separate itself. How could you leave me, given the great bond and love we share? [Surely] you see how precious and beautiful, bright, shining, and wondrous I am; how can you bear to separate yourself from me? Yes, it is true that you must continue along in your prayer in order to gather still more precious treasures and great delights, but how can you stand to cut us apart and forget me! In any case, no matter where you go, do not let us be separated, do not forget me.

And how much the more upon the conclusion of one word, the whole word now makes the same supplication, embracing and caressing [the soul], not allowing it to go further. But indeed [and alas] one is obligated to speak many words and blessings and matters until the service is complete.

For this reason one must make the whole thing into one prayer! Let each and every utterance one speaks contain within it the entire liturgy—from the beginning to the end of the service, let it all be one. When you rise and speak the final words of the service, let the first letter of the first word still reverberate. In this way, one is able to pray the entire service without separating from the very first letter of the prayers.

3. And know that such unity is the goal, as we read in Zechariah 14:9, "On that day the Lord shall be one and God's Name shall be one." "On that day," that is the goal. (1:65)

47. Rapture

התלהבות
Hitlahavut

Ecstasy

Martin Buber,
"The Life of the Hasidim: *Hitlahavut*: Ecstasy" [5]

Martin Buber (1878–1965) is arguably the most influential exponent of Jewish spirituality of the twentieth century. Buber was born in Germany but spent the formative years of his youth with his grandfather in Poland, where he experienced the ecstasy of the Hasidim firsthand. Until Buber, Hasidism had been dismissed by mainstream Jewish intellectuals as merely a vulgar, superstitious form of folk religion. Through his many writings (which have been criticized for being more Buber than Hasidism), he demonstrated the theological and spiritual depth of the movement. He brought Hasidic stories to the religious and literary attention of the West.

Martin Buber spent his last decades in Jerusalem. Asked, shortly after his emigration, how his Hebrew was coming along, he is alleged to have replied, "Good enough that I can be understood in it but yet not so good that I can't!" This passage is so beautifully poetic that it begs to be read slowly and aloud.

Hitlahavut is "the inflaming," the ardor of ecstasy. It is the goblet of grace and the eternal key. A fiery sword guards the way to the tree of life. It scatters into sparks before the touch of *hitlahavut*, whose light finger is more powerful than it. To *hitlahavut* the path is open, and all bounds sink before its boundless step. The world is no longer its place: it is the place of the world.

Hitlahavut unlocks the meaning of life. Without it even heaven has no meaning and no being. "If a man has fulfilled the whole of the teaching and all the commandments but has not had the rapture and the inflaming, when he dies and passes beyond, paradise is opened to him but, because he has not felt rapture in the world, he also does not feel it in paradise."

Hitlahavut can appear at all places and at all times. Each hour is its footstool and each deed its throne. Nothing can stand against it, nothing can hold it down; nothing can defend itself against its might, which raises everything corporeal to spirit. He who is in it is in holiness. "He can speak idle words with his mouth, yet the teaching of the Lord is in his heart at this hour; he can pray in a whisper, yet his heart cries out in his breast; he can sit in a community of men, yet he walks with God, he can allow his mouth to speak what it may speak and his ear to hear what it may hear, and he will bind the things to their higher root."

Repetition, the power which weakens and decolors so much in human life, is powerless before ecstasy, which catches fire again and again from precisely the most regular, most uniform events. Ecstasy overcame one *tsaddik* in reciting the Scriptures, each time that he reached the words,

"And God spoke." A hasidic wise man who told this to his disciples added to it, "But I think also: if one speaks in truth and one receives in truth, then one word is enough to uplift the whole world and to purge the whole world from sin." To the man in ecstasy the habitual is eternally new. A *tsaddik* stood at the window in the early morning light and trembling cried, "A few hours ago it was night and now it is day—God brings up the day!" And he was full of fear and trembling. He also said, "Every creature should be ashamed before the Creator: were he perfect, as he was destined to be, then he would be astonished and awakened and inflamed because of the renewal of the creature at each time and in each moment."

But *hitlahavut* is not a sudden sinking into eternity: it is an ascent to the infinite from rung to rung. To find God means to find the way without end. (66–68)

48. The time of the Messiah

ימות המשיח

Yemot ha-mashiach

A Human Messiah

Yaakov Yitzhak Horowitz of Lublin [6]

There are two primary ways to understand the coming of the Messiah. One sees the event as a radical transformation of, and end to, history effectuated through the presence of an emissary from the Divine. The other model, more popular among Jewish mystics, is less dramatic. Here the time of the Messiah is understood not so much as a change in the way things are but in the way we understand them. The task is one involving increasing measures of human stamina and dedication. It is within our power!

The *Hozeh*, or "Seer" of Lublin (1745–1815), is considered the father of Polish Hasidism. The founders of some of the most influential Hasidic schools—Przysucha, Kotzk, Ger, and Ropczyce—were his students. He believed that it was within the power of the *tsaddik*, or rebbe, to hasten the coming of the Messiah, but first the *tsaddik* must learn how to repair himself. The more spiritually aware he becomes, the more he realizes the enormity of the task, until finally he understands his own personal similarity to the least religious and the most sinful. (I am grateful to Dr. Nehemia Polen for calling this passage to my attention.)

> Yaakov Yitzhak of Lublin once explained the difference between the *tsaddikim* [righteous ones] of any generation and the Messiah. Every *tsaddik* spends each day in the service of God according to his level of attainment. And on the morrow he adds to the preceding day's achievement. And so it goes, each day he adds a little more. But with a *tsaddik* who is the Messiah it is different. He too must add a little more from the preceding day's accomplishments; however, over the night, everything he had achieved is erased, taken from him, so that on the next day he must start all over again from the very beginning. (58)

49. Shabbat: A taste of the world to come

מעין העולם הבא
Mei-ein ha-olam ha-ba

The Apple Orchard
Yehuda Aryeh Lieb of Ger, *Sefas Emes*[7]

Perhaps no other religious symbol in Judaism embraces more potential mystery than the Sabbath day. It is literally a mode of being into which we enter and a possibility that is set before us week after week after week. It is a taste of the messianic time.

The weekly Torah portion for this teaching is *Vayigash*, in Genesis 44:18–47:27, where Judah—still unaware that the Egyptian vizier to whom he speaks is none other than his own brother Joseph—draws near, entreating for the safety of Benjamin. The larger theme, as is so common in the thinking of Yehuda Aryeh Lieb of Ger (section 36), is the Sabbath. We today might regard the seventh day as a day for spiritual reflection and restoration but, as we shall see, for Jewish mysticism it is also an entrance into ultimate meaning. The sermon begins with a "wrinkle," an apparent redundancy, in a popular Sabbath table hymn ascribed to Isaac Luria of Safed. In Luria's hymn the apple trees (or orchard) are a metaphor for God's indwelling presence, or *Shekhinah*, which, in turn, is also *Malkhut*, the last of the ten *sefirot* (section 21).

A line in a Sabbath table hymn of Isaac Luria reads: "I will sing praises to enter into the midst of the doorway of the apple orchard." [Song of Songs 2:3, "Like an apple tree among the trees of the forest, so is my beloved among young men."] But this is odd, why say "into the midst of the doorway"? All the author of the song needed to say was "to enter into the apple orchard."

But indeed, the "apple orchard" is everywhere, as we read in Isaiah 6:3, "God's presence is the fullness of all the world." We also read in Genesis 27:27 [when Isaac thinks he is blessing his son Esau], "Note that the smell of my son is like the smell of the field [ordinary dirt]." This is precisely because the whole idea of religious service is to be open to [and aware of] this tiny point.

And on the Sabbath this gateway [to realizing God's presence everywhere] is opened, as we read in Ezekiel 46:1, "The gate of the innermost courtyard...is closed during the six days of creation, but on the Sabbath it is opened." We find a parallel from this to the Sabbath day among the days of creation: even though the Sabbath seems to be in the midst of time, nevertheless it issues like a fountain from the world to come.

And just this is the difference between the days of the week and the Sabbath, for on the Sabbath the innermost point [of God's presence within all creation] is opened. As we read in Midrash *Bereishit Rabbah* 11:2, "There is nothing like a person's countenance on the Sabbath." On the Sabbath, it's simply easier to sense the holiness. Similarly, [on the Sabbath] we are able to understand how the presence of the Holy One is everywhere—even when it's not immediately apparent. This is also the faith of every Jew in affirming God's unity. "One" here means that it's all God; God is everything!

And even though we are incapable of comprehending the full meaning of this, nevertheless, we need to believe it. Only through such faith can we arrive at ultimate truth.

It is written in another place that truth and faith are two levels. And this is what the meeting of Joseph and Judah is all about. As it is written in *Midrash Bereishit Rabbah* 93:2 (citing Job 41:8), "One [Joseph/faith] draws near to another [Judah/truth]." Similarly we read in Zechariah 14:9, "The Lord is One and God's Name is One," which implies that in the future, this unity at the core of all creation, will be clear to us.

This is also what the *Zohar* (II, 135b) means when it speaks of "the secret of unity," for now it remains concealed from us. Such divine unity is beyond our comprehension, as it is written in Isaiah 43:7, "[Then, in the future] all that is called by My Name, I have created, formed, and made for My glory," for this world was created by God's Name [even though we cannot grasp it].

And now we understand what Judah means when he entreats Joseph, "*bi adoni,* Please, my lord," for this phrase can also be read to mean, "God is in me!" And Rabbi Isaac

Luria interprets it similarly in a literal sense: The Hebrew letters of Judah's name—*yod, hey, vav, dalet,* and *hey*—literally contain the four letters of God's Ineffable Name, *yod, hey, vav,* and *hey.*

With faith that God supervises everything, each human being has the ability to be repaired—even at a time when God seems hopelessly hidden. You need only believe that the soul of the Living God is within you. As it is written of every one in Israel (in the daily prayer book), "The soul that You have set within me is pure." And through such self-annihilation and distilling oneself down to this divine point of vitality, one is able to recognize the truth.

It is revealed to him, as we find in the case of Judah's approach (Genesis 45:1), "And Joseph was unable to restrain himself." And, as it is written in another place, "In Your light." For Joseph and Judah represent, respectively, the Sabbath day and the six days of creation. In the same way, on every Sabbath day that innermost point [of the divinity of all creation] descends and becomes accessible to every one in Israel. One needs only to draw out this point [latent] within the days of creation and then be worthy on the next Sabbath to receive another spark.

50. You shall be holy. —Leviticus 19:2
קדשים תהיו

Kedoshim tehiyu

The Garden Rake

Moses Chayim Luzzatto, *Mesilat Yesharim*[8]

Moses Chayim Luzzatto was born 1707 in Italy and was widely regarded as a genius. The local rabbinic authorities, learning of his mystical teachings, became convinced he was a heretic. Luzzatto was forced to flee to Amsterdam and ultimately to Israel. At the age of 39, in 1746, he and his entire family died in a plague.

Luzzatto attained something like the status of sainthood in the eyes of Eastern European Jewry. It is difficult to overestimate the importance of his tract on ethics, *Mesilat Yesharim*, "The Path of the Righteous." In some East Europe *yeshivot* pupils were expected to memorize it! *Mesilat Yesharim* is probably the most influential ethical work in Jewish history. It describes a mystical world-view in which everything is potentially sacred. Everyone and everything is latent with holiness awaiting our touch.

The fulfillment of ethical existence is holiness. How do you brush your teeth? How do you hold the ones you love? How do you put food into your mouth? How do you handle the garden rake? Everywhere we find myriad opportunities for transforming the world around us and, through so doing, transforming ourselves.

> Even when you are engaged in the physical activities required by your body, your soul must not budge from its cleaving to the Divine.... In any deed you might perform, you do not depart or move from God. In this way even the physical objects you use actually become more elevated *because* you have used them. (326, 328)

Epilogue

Jewish Mysticism Reconsidered

A mystic believes that, beneath the apparent contradictions, brokenness, and discord of this everyday world lies a hidden divine unity. Just beyond the radar screens of our five senses, all being is one luminous organism. Religion is a system of sacred word and gesture designed to increase the likelihood we will remember that it's all one, or, as we Jews say, God is One. Or, as the Hasidim used to say, *Altz is Gott,* "It's all God!"

Consider the alternative: Can it be that reality is only what you can see and that nothing is connected to anything else? Is everything in life governed by chance, happenstance, a roll of the dice? Or, for those who believe in God's existence, is it possible that God is involved only in some things but not everything? No, for a mystic, God is not only involved in everything, God *is* everything. To borrow an ancient mystical metaphor: God is the ocean and we are the waves. The goal and the challenge of the mystic is to keep that awesome possibility ever present in one's consciousness.

We all experience fleeting glimmers of this ultimate truth—when we're with people we love and with ones we don't, during solitary walks in the forest and while caught in rush-hour traffic, in the market or at a funeral. These little epiphanies make us grateful to be human, and they invariably make us also want to be better people. There's no way to know exactly when these garden-variety mystical moments will occur. They last for only a moment or two and then, in the twinkling of an eye, they're gone. No spiritual fireworks, no

Handel's *Hallelujah* chorus sung by angels—just a fleeting reminder that everything is connected, that we are part of something much larger than ourselves, something that overrides all our carefully laid plans.

Throughout Jewish history this yearning to experience and comprehend the unity within all creation has found myriad expressions: from Sinai and the psalms of the Hebrew Bible to the teachings of mainstream mystical talmudic sages like Rabbi Akiva. It exploded again with the appearance of the *Zohar* in thirteenth-century Spain and with Rabbi Isaac Luria of Safed three hundred years later. It reappeared in the Hasidic revival of the eighteenth century and continues all the way up to the nascent spiritual revival of our own day. Each one of these flowerings of the Jewish mystical imagination has added to Judaism its own overlay of imagery, vocabulary, and rituals. Indeed, we would be hard pressed to find any aspect of Jewish life that has not incorporated mystical elements. Gershom Scholem, one of the great historians of our generation, has observed that, for centuries, the average Jew on the street probably knew more *Zohar* than Talmud! From *Lekha Dodi* (a mystical hymn) in the Sabbath evening liturgy to *tikkun olam* (a cornerstone of Lurianic Kabbalah) of political action, the influence of our mystical heritage is ubiquitous.

Balancing Rationalism and Mysticism

If this is so, then why do so many modern liberals regard mysticism with suspicion? Why has liberal Judaism effectively expunged most, if not all, references to its mystical tradition? Until recently, it was hardly mentioned in religious school textbooks. It is rarely taught even to rabbinic students. Jewish seekers often get the impression that they would do better to search out the mysticism of Eastern religions than to bother looking in the temple library. Why have the pages on Jewish mysticism been torn out of the books?

The answer, in part, can be found in our origins. Liberal Judaism is the child of German rationalism. We proudly trace our roots to Immanuel Kant and Hermann Cohen and not, for instance, to the Hasidic master Yehudah Aryeh Lieb of Ger in Poland or Abraham Isaac Kook, the first Ashkenazi chief rabbi of Israel, both of whom were towering intellects, prolific writers, *and* mystics. Our liberal predecessors dismissed East European Jewish mysticism as unenlightened, irrational, and superstitious. This bias is plainly evident, for example, in the writings of Abraham Idelsohn, the great German-trained liturgist, who asserts that "in its very essence, mysticism is a negation of life, an escape from its realities and hardships"! Heinrich Graetz, arguably the nineteenth century's most influential Jewish historian, described Hasidism (the last great flowering of Jewish mysticism) as: "a daughter of darkness...born in gloom, [that] even today proceeds stealthily on its mysterious way." Lest there be any doubt about his assessment, this teacher of our teachers put it bluntly: "Mysticism and madness are contagious."

We now suspect that our German rationalist predecessors were perhaps too overzealous in their blanket condemnation. We understand that rationalism without mysticism is sterile. Mysticism is not escapist and madness but an essential and vital ingredient of a mature and balanced Jewish world-view.

In the opinion of many, mysticism connotes renouncing the world and ethical disinterest. While that may be true of some varieties of Eastern mysticism, such thinking has never found a home among the Jews. If anything, Jewish mystics are tediously rational. Far from ignoring the world, they embrace all creation as a manifestation of the Divine. For mystics, the task is to find God's presence everywhere and then act in such a way as to help others find it, too. Ethical behavior is inseparable from and, indeed, a central expression of the Jewish mystical enterprise. We have only to consider the courageous political activism of such contemporary mystical giants as Abraham Isaac Kook in Israel, who fought tirelessly for the inclusion of all Jews—including liberals and even secularists—in the Zionist dream, or Abraham Joshua Heschel, who marched for civil rights at the side of Reverend Martin Luther King, Jr. Indeed, the definitive manuals of Jewish ethical discipline, *Mesilat Yesharim* by Moses Chayim Luzzatto and the *Shulchan Arukh* by Joseph Caro (d. 1575), were written by practicing Kabbalists!

The Jewish choice is not rationalism *or* mysticism, logic *or* spirituality, but both. Just as early Reform's categorical rejection of all ritual as superstitious resulted in an antiseptic cerebralism, so too does the renunciation of anything mystical deprive us of poetry and mystery. Indeed, without this mystical dimension, liberal Judaism of our own generation is impoverished and tepid. Core religious experience is beyond words and reason. That doesn't mean that it's antirational, spaced out, or navel contemplating, but merely that the numinous transcends logic. To put it bluntly, if you can explain it, it ain't God.

Emerging Mystical Metaphors

Permit me a few ancient, mystical metaphors that seem to have reappeared in contemporary liberal Judaism and hold high promise.

Probably the best known comes from Isaac Luria in sixteenth-century Safed, whose Kabbalah (or mystical tradition) promulgated a daring creation legend: that God underestimated the creative power of the divine light. The vessels God had prepared to receive the light shattered, leaving a world of brokenness, husks, and shards. The primordial light remains trapped, imprisoned within. The task—indeed, the purpose of—humanity is to repair creation, to free the sparks and literally put the world back together. This is called *tikkun olam*. It is much more than mere political action (although that is an indispensable element). It involves virtually everything a Jew does: through the performance of *mitzvot*, we are able to fix the world.

This brings us to a second and equally mystical metaphor: What we do in this world affects heaven. Our actions have cosmic significance. Mitzvot—even the mitzvot we do not yet understand—are not merely good deeds, or even divine obligations; they change the very workings of the universe. In the words of the kabbalists, "From awakening below comes awakening on high."

We liberal Jews share a growing sense today that the Torah—once only a document of enlightened reason—is, even more important, also an accurate manifestation of ultimate awareness. This is certainly not fundamentalism. (The *Zohar* itself says that the stories in the Torah could not possibly be about what they *seem* to be about, otherwise we could write better stories ourselves!) Rather, we are now beginning to understand that to call Torah sacred means that it is a uniquely potent mechanism for comprehending the very infrastructure of being. We may not be able to see it, but in the words of Proverbs, "She is a tree of life to those who hold fast to her." Or, to put it another way, there is more God in Torah than anyone can fathom. According to the Kabbalists, the Messiah will teach us how to pronounce the entire Torah as one long name of God.

This, in turn, leads us to another classical mystical idea: there's more to reality than meets the eye. Reality is layered, concealing myriad interrelationships and meanings. The Kabbalists went so far as to try symbolically to diagram reality or, as it were, the divine psyche itself. They envisioned a sefirotic tree (a diagram with ten circles). We today are more comfortable with the double helix of DNA or the unified field theory of modern physics, but they're all fundamentally the same: one awesomely integrated organism.

Psalm 19: One Last Reading

For the leader, a Psalm of David:
    The heavens rehearse the presence of God, just as the firmament proclaims God's doing. Day after day speaking

gushes forth, just as night after night wisdom is whispered. But of course there can be no speaking, nor can there be any words; indeed, the voices of the heavens and the firmament cannot even be heard. Still their voice reverberates throughout creation, their words to the ends of the earth. With them, God has made a tent for the sun. It is like a bridegroom emerging from his marriage canopy, like an athlete in prime, ready for the contest. He comes out at one end of the heavens and his course leads him to the other. No one can hide from the heat of the sun.

The Torah of God is really very simple, reviving the soul; the testimony of God is sure, giving wisdom to the fool. The statutes of God are right, rejoicing the heart; the commandment of God is clear, enlightening the eyes. The reverence of God is pure, enduring forever; the judgments of God are true and righteous altogether. More precious than gold, even than all the finest gold; it is sweeter than honey dripping from the comb. For this reason, your servant is eager to follow them; the reward is great.

Who could possibly be aware of every mistake? O let me be free from inadvertent wrongdoing. Keep your servant far from deliberate sins; let arrogance have no power over me. Only then will I be innocent and clear of great transgression. May these words of my mouth and the meditation of my heart be acceptable before You, O God, my rock and my redeemer.

We ask ourselves, how much God is in the world? Most of us were raised to believe that God resides beyond this world, trying benevolently (though not always successfully) to run it. In such a model, some things, some places, and some times are without the divine presence; evil, for instance, has nothing whatsoever to do with God. For mystics, on the other hand, God is everywhere and all the time. That doesn't mean mystics don't rail against injustice or try to make things better. But it does mean that even when they can't discern the presence of the Divine, mystics remain stubbornly convinced that God—the source, the ground, the font of all being—is somehow present. God is the ocean and we are the waves. *Shema Yisrael* (Deuteronomy 6:4)—"Hear O Israel, the Lord our God, the Lord is One!"

Notes

Chapter 1

1. Abraham Joshua Heschel, *God in Search of Man* (New York: Farrar, Straus and Giroux, 1955).
2. Menachem Nachum Twersky of Chernobyl, *Me'or Eina'im*, s.v. *Noah* (Brooklyn, N.Y.: 1985).
3. Kalonymous Kalman Shapira of Piesetzna, *Benei Makhshava Tovah* (Jerusalem: 1989).
4. Israel Baal Shem Tov, *Keter Shem Tov* (Jerusalem: 1968).
5. Rav Abraham Isaac Ha-Kohen Kook, *Orot Ha-Kodesh*, vol. 1 (Jerusalem: Mossad Ha-Rav Kook, 1985).

Chapter 2

1. Yechiel Michal of Zlochov, *Yosher Divrei Emet* (Jerusalem: 1974).
2. Richard L. Rubenstein, *Morality and Eros* (New York: McGraw-Hill, 1970).
3. Levi Yitzchak of Berditchev, *Kedushat Levi* (Minukad, Jerusalem).
4. Yitzchak Isaac HaLevi Epstein of Homel, "*Hanah Ariel,*" in *Seeker of Unity,* ed. Louis Jacobs (New York: Basic Books, 1966).
5. Dov Baer of Mezritch, *Maggid Devarav Le-Yaakov,* ed. Rivka Shatz-Uffenheimer (Jerusalem: Magnes Press, 1976).
6. Ibid.

Chapter 3

1. Moses ben Nachman (Nachmanides), *Commentary on the Torah,* ed. Hayim B. Chavel (Jerusalem: Mossad Ha-Rav Kook, 1959).

Chapter 4

1. Gershom Scholem, *On the Possibility of Jewish Mysticism in Our Time* (Philadelphia: Jewish Publication Society, 1997), 14.
2. Menachem Nachum Twersky of Chernobyl, *Me'or Eina'im* (Brooklyn, N.Y.: 1975).
3. *The Book of [Divine] Unity,* cited in Moshe Idel, "Infinities of Torah in Kabbalah," in *Midrash and Literature,* ed. Geoffrey H. Hartman and Sanford Budick (New Haven: Yale University Press, 1986).
4. Menachem Recanati, cited in Gershom Scholem, *On the Kabbalah and Its Symbolism,* trans. Ralph Manheim (New York: Schocken, 1965).

5. Yaakov Yosef of Polnoye, *Toledot Yaakov Yosef* (Brooklyn, N.Y.: Ateres Publishing, 1998).
6. Naftali Tsvi Horowitz of Ropczyce, *Zera Kodesh,* vol. 2 (Jerusalem: 1971).
7. Dov Baer of Mezritch, *Or Ha-Meir,* vol. 1, ed. Zev Wolf of Zhitomir (Jerusalem: 1999).

Chapter 5
1. Moshe Cordovero, *Pardes Rimonim,* sec. 4, *Atzmot v'Kaylim,* ch. 3–4 (Jerusalem: 1998).
2. Chaim Vital, *Eitz Chayim, Shaar Egolim v'Yosher,* part 2 (Jerusalem: 1975).
3. Shaul Boiman, *Miftachei Chakhmat Emet* (Warsaw: 1936).
4. Gershom Scholem, trans., "*Heikhalot Zutrati,*" in *Jewish Gnosticism, Merkabah Mysticism and Talmudic Tradition* (New York: Jewish Theological Seminary of America, 1965).

Chapter 6
1. Dov Baer of Mezritch, *Maggid Devarav Le-Yaakov,* ed. Rivka Shatz-Uffenheimer (Jerusalem: Magnes Press, 1976).
2. Ibid.
3. Citing *Siftein Tsaddikim,* s.v. *Miketz.*
4. Dov Baer of Mezritch, *Itturay Torah,* vol. 6, ed. Aaron Greenberg (Tel Aviv: Yavneh, 1978).
5. Meshullam Fiebush of Zabrash, *Yosher Divrei Emet* (Jerusalem: 1974).

Chapter 7
1. Levi Yitzhak of Berditchev, *Itturay Torah,* vol. 3, ed. Aaron Greenberg (Tel Aviv: Yavneh, 1978).
2. Alexander Altman, "God and the Self in Jewish Mysticism," *Judaism,* vol. III, no. 2, 1954.
3. Pinchas of Koretz: *Mi-Torat ha-Hasidut: Torat Rabbeinu Pinchas mi-Koretz* (Bilgoray, 1931).
4. Adin Steinsaltz, *The Thirteen Petalled Rose,* trans. Yehuda Hanegbe (New York: Basic Books, 1980).
5. Dov Baer of Mezritch, *Likkutim Yekarim* (Jerusalem: 1971).
6. Yehuda Aryeh Lieb of Ger, *Sefas Emes,* s.v. *Bamidbar,* 5631.
7. Moses Cordovero, *Pardes Rimonim,* vol. 4, fol. 23c, cited in Moshe Idel, *Kabbalah: New Perspectives* (New London, Conn.: Yale University Press, 1988).
8. Gershom Scholem, *Major Trends in Jewish Mysticism* (Jerusalem: Schocken, 1941).
9. Ibid., 256

Chapter 8
1. Chaim Vital, *Shaar haMitzvot,* s.v. *Vaethanan,* 78, cited by Moshe Idel, *Kabbalah: New Perspectives* (New London, Conn.: Yale University Press, 1988).

2. Dov Baer of Mezritch, *Tzava'at ha-Rivash* (Brooklyn, N.Y.: Kehot Publication Society, 1998).
3. Menachem Mendl of Vitebsk, *P'ri ha-Aretz* (Jerusalem: 1989).
4. Alexander Susskind, *Yesod ve-Shoresh ha-Avodah*, vol. 2; *Shaar Ha-Kolel*, vol. 2, ch. 3 (Jerusalem: 1987).
5. Menachem Mendl Krengel, *Devash ve-chalav* (Cracow: 1910) in *Itturay Torah*, vol. 1, ed. Aaron Greenberg (Tel Aviv: Yavneh, 1978).
6. Isaac ben Chaim of Vlozhyn, *Nefesh ha-chayim*, gate 1, ch. 6.
7. Kalonymous Kalman Epstein of Cracow, *Ma'or va-Shemesh*, vol. 1 (Jerusalem: 1992).

Chapter 9
1. Menachem Mendl Morgenstern of Kotzk, *Itturay Torah*, vol. 1, ed. Aaron Greenberg (Tel Aviv: Yavneh, 1976).
2. Zev Wolf of Zhitomir, *Or ha-Meir*, vol. 1 (Jerusalem: 1998).
3. Dov Baer of Mezritch, *Tzava'at ha-Rivash* (Brooklyn, N.Y.: Kehot Publication Society, 1998).
4. Elijah de Vidas, *Reishit Chokhmah*, vol. 1 (1579), sec. 4, ch. 4.
5. Martin Buber, "The Life of the Hasidim: *Hitlahavut*: Ecstasy," in *Hasidism and Modern Man*, ed. and trans. Maurice Friedman (Atlantic Highlands, N.J.: Humanities Press International, 1988).
6. Yaakov Yitzhak Horowitz of Lublin (Jerusalem: 1987).
7. Yehuda Aryeh Lieb of Ger, *Sefas Emes*, s.v. *Yayigash*, 5635.
8. Moses Chaim Luzzatto, *Mesilat Yesharim* (New York: Feldheim Publishers, 1969).

Glossary

Sometimes two pronunciations of words are common. This glossary reflects the way that many Jews actually use these words, not just the technically correct version. When two pronunciations are listed, the first is the way the word is sounded in proper Hebrew, and the second is the way it is sometimes heard in common speech, often under the influence of Yiddish, the folk language of the Jews of northern and eastern Europe. "Kh" is used to represent a guttural sound, similar to the German "ch" (as in "sprach").

Adam Qadmon (ah-DAHM kad-MOHN): The primordial human archetype (not to be confused with *Adam haRishon*, the first Adam of the Garden of Eden). A cosmic template of the primal and ultimate human form. Also, a halfway image between *Ayn Sof*, the unknowable, infinite unity of God and everyday reality.

ahtbash: A system of Hebrew letter rearrangement wherein the first letter of the alphabet, *aleph*, is replaced with the last letter, *tav*—hence, *aht*, and the second letter, *bet*, is exchanged with the second from the last letter, *shin*—hence, *bahsh*, and so on.

Ayin (ah-YIN): "Nothingness," but not the absence of being. The absence of any "thingness," definition or boundary, therefore, boundless, without beginning, without end; another name for eternity. A no "thing," a nothing that encompasses all creation and therefore the font of all being, the substrate of creation.

bittul yesh (b'TOOL YEHSH): The negation of what is; the annihilation of selfhood. Attained through the total absorption in and devotion to serving God.

Continuous Creation: A Hasidic doctrine maintaining that God's creation of the world is not an event that happened in the past but something present at this moment. Without God's continuous creative power each and every minute, creation would revert to primordial chaos.

devekut (d'-vay-KOOT): Communion with, cleaving to, or fusion with God. The ultimate goal of Jewish spirituality. *Unio mystica*. To be present within the Divine.

halakhah (hah-LAH-khah): Jewish law. From the Hebrew meaning "to walk, to go," thus the way on which a person should walk through life.

Hasidism (KHAH-sihd-ihsm): An ecstatic, spiritual folk revival of mid-eighteenth-century Poland founded by the Baal Shem Tov (or the BeSHT) preaching joy, communion with God, and devotion to one's rebbe or spiritual master.

hishtavut (hish-tah-VOOT): Equanimity. An attitude toward whatever happens, good or bad, that it must all somehow be "from" God and therefore be accepted with an even spirit. From the Hebrew root meaning "to be equal."

hitlahavut (hit-lah-hah-VOOT): Religious ecstasy, fervor; a self-reflexive form of the Hebrew root "to set on fire," hence, self-ignition.

Kabbalah (kah-bah-LAH or, commonly, kah-BAH-lah): A thirteenth-century Spanish system of theosophy explaining the inner workings of the divine psyche and the significance of human action. The doctrine is built around the dynamic structure of God as envisioned in the *Ayn Sof* and *sefirot* and its relationship with human beings through the performance of sacred deeds.

Kabbalat Shabbat (kah-bah-LAHT shah-BAHT): Welcoming the Sabbath. The liturgy initiating the Sabbath that is recited on Friday evenings at sunset.

Kudsha Barikh Hu (KUHD-shah b'-REEKH HOO): Aramaic for *HaKadosh Barukh Hu* (hah-kah-DOSH bah-ROOKH HOO) An epithet for God; literally, "The Holy One, Blessed be He."

Lurianic Kabbalah: A form of Kabbalah developed by Isaac Luria in sixteenth-century Safed. It focuses on God's self-withdrawl *(tsimtsum)* from the universe to make space for creation, the unanticipated "shattering of the vessels" *(sh'virat haKaylim)* resulting in the discord of creation and "repairing the world" *(tikkun olam)*, which is humanity's sacred task and goal.

machshavot zarot (mahkh-shah-VOHT zah-ROHT): Hasidism's doctrine of "alien thoughts" during prayer which understands distracting and even shameful thoughts occurring to the worshiper, not as foreign, but instead as dimensions of the worshiper's personality. Sensing this prayerful moment, they have arisen from the depths of the psyche seeking redemption.

merkavah (mehr-KAH-vah): The chariot of Ezekiel's vision; the paradigm Jewish mystical experience.

midrash (meed-RAHSH or, commonly, MID-rahsh): From the Hebrew, *drash*, "to seek, search, or examine" [meaning from the biblical text]; hence, a literary genre focused on drawing new meaning from the Bible text. Also, any literature that offers interpretations of the Bible.

mitzvah (meetz-VAH or, commonly, MITZ-vah); pl. *mitzvot* (meetz-VOHT): A divine commandment; what God wants us to do.

Mysticism: A form of religious expression built around the notion that the apparent discord, contradictions and brokenness of the world conceal a hidden and ultimate unity, and that it is possible for the devout to fleetingly become one with that ultimate unity.

parasha (pah-rah-SHAH); pl. *parshiyot* (pahr-shee-YOHT): One of 54 weekly lections from the **Torah**, or Five Books of Moses, read in the synagogue. Hence, a classic thematic organizing structure for Jewish thought.

PaRDeS (pahr-DAYS): Literally, "orchard" or "garden"; also serves as an acronym for the four layers of meaning within each word of the biblical text: *peshat,* the simple, superficial, obvious meaning; *remez,* the hinted at, associational meaning; *derash,* the interpreted and expounded meaning; and *sod,* the secret, mystical meaning.

sefirot (seh-fee-ROHT): Literally, "numbers," or manifestations or emanations of God's creative process. Frequently portrayed as ten concentric circles or "spheres" (but this has no relation to the Hebrew *sefira,* which only means "number"). The *sefirot* are the closest we can come to comprehending the inner workings, the psyche of the God. They are the infrastructure of being. To understand them and their interaction is to comprehend ultimate reality.

Shabbat (shah-BAHT): Sabbath.

Shem ha-Meforash (SHAYM hah-m'-foh-RAHSH): The Explicit or Ineffable Name of God; the Tetragramaton; made from the four Hebrew letters *yod, hey, vav* and *hey,* the same root letters as the Hebrew verb "to be." It probably originally meant "The One who brings into being all that is." Unpronounceable, both out of reverence and because it is made from only vowels and therefore often incorrectly transliterated as *Yahweh.*

Shekhinah (sh'-khee-NAH or, commonly, sh'-KHEE-nah): God's feminine, indwelling Presence; also the bottom and most easily accessible of the ten *sefirot.*

siddur (see-DOOR or, commonly, SIH-d'r): The traditional Jewish prayerbook; from the Hebrew *seder,* meaning, order, and therefore, the "order" of prayers.

sitra achra (siht-RAH ahkh-RAH): Aramaic, literally, "the other side;" "the Dark side of the Force," the daemonic side of creation and the psyche. Nevertheless, a manifestation of God's power.

Talmud (tahl-MOOD or, commonly, TAHL-m'd): The two great compendia of Jewish law and legend compiled between the second and sixth centuries; hence, the literary core of rabbinic Judaism. One Talmud was compiled in the land of Israel, the *Talmud Yerushalmi* (y'-roo-SHAHL-mee), or "Jerusalem Talmud." The, other, better-known Talmud was compiled in Babylonia, hence *Talmud Bavli* (BAHV-lee), or "Babylonian Talmud."

TaNaKh (tah-NAHKH): An acronym derived from the initial letters of the three parts of the Hebrew Bible: Torah (Way or Law), *Nevi'im* (Prophets), and *Ketuvim* (Writings).

teshuvah (t'-shoo-VAH): Often translated as repentance but more importantly, a primary religious gesture; a willingness to die and become one again with one's creator. The source of all sacred deeds.

tikkun olam (t'-KOON oh-LAHM): Literally, "repairing the world;" according to Lurianic Kabbalah, the primary task of humanity.

Torah (TOH-rah): Literally, "teaching" or "way"; also known as the Five Books of Moses, or the *Chumash*, (khoo-MAHSH). By extension, all Jewish sacred literature—the Bible, midrash, the Talmud, and all the commentaries.

tsaddik (tsah-DEEK): An extraordinarily righteous person.

yesh: "Somethingness" or "isness;" and by extension, all the created world.

Zohar: (ZOH-hahr): Literally, radiance or splendor. The central text of Kabbalah; a pseudopigraphic collection of dozens of different commentaries and *midrashim* on the Torah and attributed to the second-century mystic Shimon bar Yochai but actually composed in Spain at the end of the thirteenth century by Moshe de Leon.

Suggestions for Further Reading

Blumenthal, David R. *Understanding Jewish Mysticism: A Source Reader.* Vol. 1, *The Merkavah Tradition and the Zoharic Tradition.* New York: KTAV, 1978.

Blumenthal, David R. *Understanding Jewish Mysticism: A Source Reader.* Vol. 2, *The Philosophic-Mystical Tradition and the Hasidic Tradition.* New York: KTAV, 1982.

Bokser, Ben Zion, trans. *Abraham Isaac Kook: The Lights of Penitence, Lights of Holiness, the Moral Principles, Essays, Letters, and Poems.* Ramsey, N.J.: Paulist Press, 1978.

Buber, Martin. *Hasidism and Modern Man.* Transliterated and edited by Maurice Friedman. Atlantic Highlands, N.J.: Humanities Press International, 1988. (More Buber than Hasidism, a rich and evocative anthology of Jewish spirituality.)

Cohen, Norman J. *The Way Into Torah.* Woodstock, Vt.: Jewish Lights, 2000.

Dan, Joseph. *The Ancient Jewish Mysticism.* Tel Aviv: MOD Books, 1993. (Distributed in the United States by Jewish Lights Publishing, Woodstock, Vt.)

Fine, Lawrence, ed. *Essential Papers on Kabbalah.* New York: New York University Press, 1995.

Fine, Lawrence. "Kabbalistic Texts." In *Back to the Sources: Reading the Classic Jewish Texts,* edited by Barry W. Holtz. New York: Summit Books, 1984.

Fine, Lawrence, ed. and trans. *Safed Spirituality: Rules of Mystical Piety, the Beginning of Wisdom.* Ramsey, N.J.: Paulist Press, 1984.

Fishbane, Michael. *The Kiss of God: Spiritual and Mystical Death in Judaism.* Seattle, Wash.: University of Washington Press, 1994.

Gillman, Neil. *The Way Into Encountering God in Judaism.* Woodstock, Vt.: Jewish Lights, 2000.

Ginsburg, Elliot K. *The Sabbath in the Classical Kabbalah.* Albany, N.Y.: State University Press of New York, 1989.

Green, Arthur. "The Aleph-Bet of Creation: Jewish Mysticism for Beginners." *Tikkun* 7, no. 4: p. 45.

Green, Arthur, trans. *The Language of Truth: The Torah Commentary of the Sefat Emet, Rabbi Yehudah Lieb Alter of Ger.* Philadelphia: Jewish Publication Society, 1998.

Green, Arthur and Barry W. Holtz. *Your Word Is Fire: The Hasidic Masters on Contemplative Prayer.* Woodstock, Vt.: Jewish Lights, 1993.

Heschel, Abraham J. "The Mystical Element in Judaism." In *The Jews: Their History, Culture, and Religion*. Edited by Louis Finkelstein. Vol. 2. Westport, Conn.: Greenwood Press, 1949.

Hoffman, Lawrence A. *The Way Into Jewish Prayer*. Woodstock, Vt.: Jewish Lights, 2000.

Idel, Moshe. *Hasidism: Between Ecstasy and Magic*. Albany, N.Y.: State University of New York Press, 1995.

Idel, Moshe. *Kabbalah: New Perspectives*. New Haven: Yale University Press, 1988.

Jacobs, Louis. *Jewish Mystical Testimonies*. New York: Schocken, 1977.

Jacobs, Louis, trans. *The Palm Tree of Deborah*. London: Vallentine, Mitchell, 1960.

Jacobs, Louis. *Seeker of Unity: The Life and Works of Aaron of Starosselje*. New York: Basic Books, 1966.

Jacobs, Louis, trans. *Tract on Ecstasy*. London: Vallentine, Mitchell, 1963.

Kushner, Lawrence. *Honey from the Rock: An Introduction to Jewish Mysticism*, Special Anniversary Edition. Woodstock, Vt.: Jewish Lights, 2000.

Kushner, Lawrence. *The River of Light: Jewish Mystical Awareness*, Special Anniversary Edition. Woodstock, Vt.: Jewish Lights, 2000.

Luzzatto, Moshe Chaim. *Mesilat Yesharim: The Path of the Just*. Translated by Shraga Silverstein. New York: Feldheim, 1969.

Matt, Daniel C. *The Essential Kabbalah: The Heart of Jewish Mysticism*. San Francisco: HarperSanFrancisco, 1995. (An anthology of short, poetically rendered primary mystical texts.)

Matt, Daniel C. *God & the Big Bang: Discovering Harmony Between Science and Spirituality*. Woodstock, Vt.: Jewish Lights, 1996.

Matt, Daniel C., ed. and trans. *Zohar: The Book of Enlightenment*. Ramsey, N.J.: Paulist Press, 1983.

Polen, Nehemia. *The Holy Fire: The Teachings of Rabbi Kalonymus Kalman Shapira, the Rebbe of the Warsaw Ghetto*. Northvale, N.J.: Jason Aronson, 1994.

Rapaport-Albert, Ada, ed. *Hasidism Reappraised*. London: Littman Library of Jewish Civilization, 1996.

Schatz-Uffenheimer, Rivka. *Hasidism as Mysticism: Quietistic Elements in Eighteenth-Century Hasidic Thought*. Translated by Jonathan Chipman. Princeton, N.J., and Jerusalem: Princeton University Press and Magnes Press, 1993.

Scholem, Gershom. *Kabbalah*. New York and Jerusalem: Quadrangle and Keter, 1974.

Scholem, Gershom. *Major Trends in Jewish Mysticism*. New York: Schocken, 1941.

Scholem, Gershom. *The Messianic Idea in Judaism and Other Essays on Jewish Spirituality*. New York: Schocken, 1971.

Scholem, Gershom. *On the Kabbalah and Its Symbolism*. Translated by Ralph Manheim. New York: Schocken, 1965. (Five scholarly essays by the master.)

Scholem, Gershom. *On the Mystical Shape of the Godhead.* Translated by Joachim Neugroschel. New York: Schocken, 1991.

Scholem, Gershom. *Origins of the Kabbalah.* Edited by R. J. Zwi Werblowsky. Translated by Allan Arkush. Philadelphia: Jewish Publication Society, 1962.

Tishby, Isaiah, and Lachower Fischel. *The Wisdom of the Zohar: An Anthology of Texts.* 3 vols. Translated by David Goldstein. Oxford: Oxford University Press, 1989.

Weiss, Joseph. *Studies in Eastern European Jewish Mysticism.* Edited by David Goldstein. Oxford: Oxford University Press, 1985.

Index

Kabbalah mysticism. *See also*
Hasidic mysticism; Lurianic
Kabbalah; *Sefirot,* sefirotic system; *Zohar: Adam Qadmon,*
74–75, 85, 117–118; *ahtbash*
text reading, 24–25; *Asiyah,*
world of, 83–85; *Atzilut,* world
of, 83–85; *Beriyah,* world of,
83–85; color of water, 80–81;
dangers and seductions of,
94–96; four worlds, 84–85;
human body correspondance,
85; inverted tree, 72–73; meditative techniques and devotions, use of, 85–86; *Petach
Eliyahu,* 78–80; rationalism
and mysticism, balancing,
158–160; reality, layered, 161;
secret wisdom of, 103–104;
Sefer HaBahir, 72–73; *Yetzirah,*
world of, 83–85
Kabbalat Shabbat, origin of, 43
Kabbalistic literature. *See also
Zohar,* "Book of Radiance":
*Major Trends in Jewish
Mysticism,* 118; *Miftakhei
Chakhmat Emet* (Boiman),
84–85; *Pardes Rimonim,*
117–118; *Sefer ha-Yetzirah,*
73–76; *Sefer HaBahir,* 72–73,
90; *The Book of [Divine] Unity,*
57; *Tikkunei ha-Zohar,* 78–80;
Yosher Divrei Emet, 103–104
Kalonymous Kalman Epstein of
Crakow, 133–135
Kalonymus Kalman Shapira of
Piesetzna, 12–13
Kant, Immanuel, 159
Kavod (presence, glory), 9
Kelipot and *nitzozot,* 120–121
Keter (Ayin), 75, 77, 79
Kimelman, Reuven, 43
Kotzker Rebbe (Menachem Mendl
Morgenstern of Kotsk),
138–139

L

Lekha Dodi, 42–46
Levi Yitzchak of Berditchev,
21–25, 32
Liberal Judaism, 159
Light, divine: *Adam Qadmon,*
74–75, 85, 117–118; and
Lurianic Kabbalah, 160; and
Shekhinah, 90; creation, 89;
Luria view, 89; metaphor for
human conciousness, 87;
omnipresence of, 14–16; *Or
zarua,* 89; place of, 90; *Sefer
HaBahir,* 90; ultimate awareness, 88–90
Love, 52–54, 79
Love and spiritual ecstasy, 42,
51–52
Lubavitch Hasidism, 27–28
Luria, Isaac, 3, 4, 23, 81–82, 104,
119–120, 132, 153, 154–155
Lurianic Kabbalah. *See also
Zohar:* acrostics, 43; apple
orchard, 153–155; *Ayn Sof,*
18, 19, 36–37, 75, 81–84,
97–98; creation, 160; *Eitz
Chayim,* 77, 82, 161; *kelipot*
and *nitzozot,* 120–121; *Lekha
Dodi,* 42–46; princess and the
bathhouse, 143–145; shabbat,
153–155; *Shekhinah,* 44, 153;
shevirat ha-keilim, 120–121;
tikkun olam, 119–121;
tsimtzum, 29, 81–84, 118,
120–121
Lurianic Kabbalah literature. *See
also Zohar: Daily Prayerbook,*
42–46; *Eitz Chayim, Shaar
Egolim v'Yosher,* 81–84; *Pardes
Rimonim,* 80–81; *Reishit
Chokhmah,* 143–145; *Sefer ha-
Yetzirah,* 73–76; *Sefer
Haredim,* 46–47; *Shaar ha-
Yihudim,* 132; *Shaar
haMitzvot,* 119–121

M

Maimomides, 130
Major Trends in Jewish Mysticism (Scholem), 118
Malkhut, 30, 76, 77, 79
Masculine loving, 79
Matt, Daniel, 76, 88
Meditation, 104; and prayer, 124; techniques and devotions, use of, 85–86
Menachem Mendl Krengel, 129–130
Menachem Mendl Morgenstern of Kotsk, 138–139
Menachem Mendl of Permishlan, 104
Menachem Mendl of Vitebsk, 32, 127–128
Menachem Nachum Twersky of Chernobyl, 11–12, 56–57
Menachem Recanati, 57
Mendl of Rymanov, Rabbi, 66
Merkavah, 90–93, 95, 132, 133
Merkavah mystics, 3, 90, 91, 94
Meshullam Feibush of Zabrazh, 18
Messiah, time of, 151–152
Midrashic interpretations: *aleph* and face-to-face communication, 66–68; *Bereishit,* 59–61; *merkavah,* 86, 90–93, 95
Miracles, Nachmanides view on, 10
Mistakes and wrongdoing, 2
Mitzvot, significance of, 160–161
Monism of God, 25–27
Monism, radical, 28
Morality and Eros (Rubenstein), 20–21
Moses ben Nachman, Rabbi. *See* Nachmanides.
Moses ben Shem Tov de Leon, 36
Moses Chayim Luzzatto, 155–156
Moses Cordovero, 117–118, 120, 143
Mystical literature. *See also* Hasidic literature; Kabbalistic literature; Lurianic kabbalistic literature: *God in Search of Man,* 9–11; *Orot Ha-Kodesh,* 14–16
Mystical metaphors. *See also Ayin and Yesh:* Abraham's encounter with the angels, 129; apple orchard, 152–155; Birth of Isaac, 33–34; castle of illusions, 13–14; color of water, 80–81; Elijah and God's voice, 61–62; garden rake, 155–156; king, making requests, 114; light, divine, 160; ocean waves, 18–21; orchard of awareness, 94—96; orchard of souls, 145–149; *PaRDeS,* 94; prince, seduction of, 98–99; princess and the bathhouse, 143–145; *shiur koma,* 3; silver, fusing, 127–128; Sinai, the silence of, 61–63; tears of a girl, 103; tree of life, 72–73, 77, 79, 82, 161; woman in a palace, 52–54
Mysticism and rationalism, balancing, 158–160
Mysticism, Jewish. *See also* Hasidic mysticism; Kabbalah mysticism; Lurianic Kabbalah mysticism; Mystics: grammar, mystical, 28–29; Heschel's view, 9–11; historical eras of, 3; Nachmanides' view, 10
Mystics: *ahtbash* text reading, 24–25; grammar, mystical, 28–29; *Heikhalot,* 3, 85–86; *merkavah,* 3, 91, 94

N

Nachman of Bratslav, 128, 145–149
Nachmanides, 10, 34, 38–41
Naftali Tsvi Horowitz of Ropczyce, 65–68
Names of God, 36–37; 72, 216-letter name of God, 39–41; *Ayn Sof,* 36–37; Ineffable Name of

Shavuot, 91
Shekhinah, 44, 76, 90, 97–98, 103, 124, 126, 153
Shelomo Ha-Levi Alkabetz, 42–43
Shelomo, Rabbi. *See* Rashi.
Shem ha-meForash, 37–38
Shem ha-Vayah, 37–38
Shevirat ha-keilim, 120–121
Shimon, Rabbi, 36–37, 54–55
Shiur koma metaphor, 3
Sinai, silence of, 61–63
Song of Songs, 42–46
Spritual ecstasy and love, 42, 51–52
Steinsaltz, Rabbi Adin, 110–111
Suffering, response to, 142
Susskind, Alexander, 128–129

T
Tanchuma, Rabbi, 64
Tefillin, 79
Ten utterances, 37–38
Terror, meaningless of, 102
Teshuvah, 110–111
The Guide to the Perplexed (Maimomides), 130
The Life of the Hasidim: Hitlahavut: Ecstasy (Buber), 149–151
The Thirteen Petalled Rose (Steinsaltz), 110–111
Tiferet, 76, 77, 79
Tikkun leil Shavuot, origin of, 43
Tikkun olam, 119–121
Torah. *See also* Midrashic interpretations; mystical metaphors: and truth, 51; as names of God, 38–41; as woman in a palace, 52–54; black fire on white fire, 41; Body of God, mystical, 57; commandments, mysteries of, 132; *derashah* and *aggadah,* 53–54; divine word, multiple meanings for, 63–65; Ezekiel's vision of the chariot, 90–93, 95; God's voice and communication, 61–68; Hebrew letters significance, 56–59; lost letters of, 58–59; magical potential of, 55–56; *parashiyot,* hidden order of, 55–56; romantic intimacy of, 42–46, 51–54; scriptual stories interpretation, 54–55; speaking Torah, 68–69; ten utterances, 37–38; universe blueprint, 59–61; *Zohar* views on, 51–55
Torah *lishmah,* 58–59
Tree of Life, 72–73, 77, 79, 82, 161
Tsimtzum, 29, 81–84, 118, 120–121

U
Unity of God monism, 25–27

W
Weeping, 112
Wiesel, Elie, 110
Wisdom, secret, 103–104
Word of God concept, 51
World of speech *(olam ha-dibbur),* 56

Y
Yaakov Yitzchak Horowitz haHozeh (Seer of Lublin), 151–152
Yaakov Yosef of Polnoye, 11, 14, 58–59
Yearning, 137
Yechiel Michal of Zlochov, 18–20
Yedid Nefesh, 46–48
Yehuda Aryeh Lieb of Ger, 114–117, 152–155
Yesod, 76, 79
Yetzirah, world of, 83–85
Yitzchak Isaac Halevi Epstein of Homel, 25–27
Yochanan, Rabbi, 63
Yordei merkavah mysticism, 3

Z

Ze'ev Wolf of Zhitomir, 32, 69

Zohar, "Book of Radiance." *See also* Light, divine; *Sefirot,* sefirotic system: and *Tikkunei ha-Zohar,* 78–80; *Ayn Sof,* 36–37; divine needs, fulfilling, 133; evil, 98–99; Hebew letters, significance of, 28–29; hidden wisdom, 104; Ineffable Name, 37–38; light, Divine, 87–90; Name of God, 132, 133; scriptual stories interpretation, 52–55; *sitra achra,* 98–99; Torah commandments, mysteries of, 132; Torah stories, meaning of, 161; Torah, truth of, 51–55; unity, secret of, 154

Notes

Notes

Notes

Notes

Notes

Notes

Notes

Notes

Notes

Notes

AVAILABLE FROM BETTER BOOKSTORES.
TRY YOUR BOOKSTORE FIRST.

Bar/Bat Mitzvah

The JGirl's Guide: The Young Jewish Woman's Handbook for Coming of Age
By Penina Adelman, Ali Feldman, and Shulamit Reinharz
An inspirational, interactive guidebook designed to help pre-teen Jewish girls address the spiritual, educational, and psychological issues surrounding coming of age in today's society. 6 x 9, 240 pp, Quality PB, ISBN 1-58023-215-9 **$14.99**
  Also Available: **The JGirl's Teacher's and Parent's Guide**
  8½ x 11, 56 pp, PB, ISBN 1-58023-225-6 **$8.99**

Bar/Bat Mitzvah Basics: A Practical Family Guide to Coming of Age Together
By Helen Leneman 6 x 9, 240 pp, Quality PB, ISBN 1-58023-151-9 **$18.95**
The Bar/Bat Mitzvah Memory Book: An Album for Treasuring the Spiritual Celebration
By Rabbi Jeffrey K. Salkin and Nina Salkin
8 x 10, 48 pp, Deluxe Hardcover, 2-color text, ribbon marker, ISBN 1-58023-111-X **$19.95**
For Kids—Putting God on Your Guest List: How to Claim the Spiritual Meaning of Your Bar or Bat Mitzvah *By Rabbi Jeffrey K. Salkin*
6 x 9, 144 pp, Quality PB, ISBN 1-58023-015-6 **$14.99** *For ages 11–12*
Putting God on the Guest List, 3rd Edition: How to Reclaim the Spiritual Meaning of Your Child's Bar or Bat Mitzvah *By Rabbi Jeffrey K. Salkin*
6 x 9, 224 pp, Quality PB, ISBN 1-58023-222-1 **$16.99**; Hardcover, ISBN 1-58023-260-4 **$24.99**
  Also Available: **Putting God on the Guest List Teacher's Guide**
  8½ x 11, 48 pp, PB, ISBN 1-58023-226-4 **$8.99**

Tough Questions Jews Ask: A Young Adult's Guide to Building a Jewish Life
By Rabbi Edward Feinstein 6 x 9, 160 pp, Quality PB, ISBN 1-58023-139-X **$14.99** *For ages 13 & up*
  Also Available: **Tough Questions Jews Ask Teacher's Guide**
  8½ x 11, 72 pp, PB, ISBN 1-58023-187-X **$8.95**

Bible Study/Midrash

Hineini in Our Lives: Learning How to Respond to Others through 14 Biblical Texts, and Personal Stories *By Norman J. Cohen* 6 x 9, 240 pp, Quality PB, ISBN 1-58023-274-4 **$16.99**; Hardcover, ISBN 1-58023-131-4 **$23.95**
Ancient Secrets: Using the Stories of the Bible to Improve Our Everyday Lives
By Rabbi Levi Meier, Ph.D. 5½ x 8½, 288 pp, Quality PB, ISBN 1-58023-064-4 **$16.95**
Moses—The Prince, the Prophet: His Life, Legend & Message for Our Lives
By Rabbi Levi Meier, Ph.D. 6 x 9, 224 pp, Quality PB, ISBN 1-58023-069-5 **$16.95**
Self, Struggle & Change: Family Conflict Stories in Genesis and Their Healing Insights for Our Lives *By Norman J. Cohen* 6 x 9, 224 pp, Quality PB, ISBN 1-879045-66-4 **$18.99**
Voices from Genesis: Guiding Us through the Stages of Life *By Norman J. Cohen*
6 x 9, 192 pp, Quality PB, ISBN 1-58023-118-7 **$16.95**

Hineini
in Our Lives

Congregation Resources

Becoming a Congregation of Learners: Learning as a Key to Revitalizing Congregational Life *By Isa Aron, Ph.D. Foreword by Rabbi Lawrence A. Hoffman.*
6 x 9, 304 pp, Quality PB, ISBN 1-58023-089-X **$19.95**
Finding a Spiritual Home: How a New Generation of Jews Can Transform the American Synagogue *By Rabbi Sidney Schwarz*
6 x 9, 352 pp, Quality PB, ISBN 1-58023-185-3 **$19.95**
Jewish Pastoral Care, 2nd Edition: A Practical Handbook from Traditional & Contemporary Sources *Edited by Rabbi Dayle A. Friedman*
6 x 9, 464 pp, Hardcover, ISBN 1-58023-221-3 **$40.00**
The Self-Renewing Congregation: Organizational Strategies for Revitalizing Congregational Life *By Isa Aron, Ph.D. Foreword by Dr. Ron Wolfson.*
6 x 9, 304 pp, Quality PB, ISBN 1-58023-166-7 **$19.95**

Becoming
a
Congregation
of
Learners

Isa Aron, Ph.D.

Or phone, fax, mail or e-mail to: **JEWISH LIGHTS Publishing**
Sunset Farm Offices, Route 4 • P.O. Box 237 • Woodstock, Vermont 05091
Tel: (802) 457-4000 • Fax: (802) 457-4004 • www.jewishlights.com
Credit card orders: **(800) 962-4544** (8:30AM–5:30PM ET Monday–Friday)
Generous discounts on quantity orders. SATISFACTION GUARANTEED. Prices subject to change.

Children's Books

What You Will See Inside a Synagogue
By Rabbi Lawrence A. Hoffman and Dr. Ron Wolfson; Full-color photos by Bill Aron

A colorful, fun-to-read introduction that explains the ways and whys of Jewish worship and religious life. Full-page photos; concise but informative descriptions of the objects used, the clergy and laypeople who have specific roles, and much more. For ages 6 & up.

8½ x 10½, 32 pp, Full-color photos, Hardcover, ISBN 1-59473-012-1 **$17.99** *(A SkyLight Paths book)*

Because Nothing Looks Like God
By Lawrence and Karen Kushner

What is God like? Introduces children to the possibilities of spiritual life. Real-life examples of happiness and sadness invite us to explore, together with our children, the questions we all have about God.

11 x 8½, 32 pp, Full-color illus., Hardcover, ISBN 1-58023-092-X **$16.95** *For ages 4 & up*

Also Available: **Because Nothing Looks Like God Teacher's Guide**
8½ x 11, 22 pp, PB, ISBN 1-58023-140-3 **$6.95** *For ages 5–8*

Board Book Companions to *Because Nothing Looks Like God*
5 x 5, 24 pp, Full-color illus., SkyLight Paths Board Books *For ages 0–4*

What Does God Look Like? ISBN 1-893361-23-3 **$7.95**

How Does God Make Things Happen? ISBN 1-893361-24-1 **$7.95**

Where Is God? ISBN 1-893361-17-9 **$7.99**

The 11th Commandment: Wisdom from Our Children
By The Children of America

"If there were an Eleventh Commandment, what would it be?" Children of many religious denominations across America answer in their own drawings and words.

8 x 10, 48 pp, Full-color illus., Hardcover, ISBN 1-879045-46-X **$16.95** *For all ages*

Jerusalem of Gold: Jewish Stories of the Enchanted City
Retold by Howard Schwartz. Full-color illus. by Neil Waldman.

A beautiful and engaging collection of historical and legendary stories for children. Based on Talmud, midrash, Jewish folklore, and mystical and Hasidic sources.

8 x 10, 64 pp, Full-color illus., Hardcover, ISBN 1-58023-149-7 **$18.95** *For ages 7 & up*

The Book of Miracles: A Young Person's Guide to Jewish Spiritual Awareness
By Lawrence Kushner. All-new illustrations by the author.

6 x 9, 96 pp, 2-color illus., Hardcover, ISBN 1-879045-78-8 **$16.95** *For ages 9–13*

In Our Image: God's First Creatures
By Nancy Sohn Swartz

9 x 12, 32 pp, Full-color illus., Hardcover, ISBN 1-879045-99-0 **$16.95** *For ages 4 & up*

Also Available as a Board Book: **How Did the Animals Help God?**
5 x 5, 24 pp, Board, Full-color illus., ISBN 1-59473-044-X **$7.99** *For ages 0–4 (A SkyLight Paths book)*

From SKYLIGHT PATHS PUBLISHING

Becoming Me: A Story of Creation
By Martin Boroson. Full-color illus. by Christopher Gilvan-Cartwright.

Told in the personal "voice" of the Creator, a story about creation and relationship that is about each one of us.

8 x 10, 32 pp, Full-color illus., Hardcover, ISBN 1-893361-11-X **$16.95** *For ages 4 & up*

Ten Amazing People: And How They Changed the World
By Maura D. Shaw. Foreword by Dr. Robert Coles. Full-color illus. by Stephen Marchesi.

Black Elk • Dorothy Day • Malcolm X • Mahatma Gandhi • Martin Luther King, Jr. • Mother Teresa • Janusz Korczak • Desmond Tutu • Thich Nhat Hanh • Albert Schweitzer.

8½ x 11, 48 pp, Full-color illus., Hardcover, ISBN 1-893361-47-0 **$17.95** *For ages 7 & up*

Where Does God Live? *By August Gold and Matthew J. Perlman*

Helps young readers develop a personal understanding of God.

10 x 8½, 32 pp, Full-color photo illus., Quality PB, ISBN 1-893361-39-X **$8.99** *For ages 3–6*

Children's Books
by Sandy Eisenberg Sasso

Adam & Eve's First Sunset: God's New Day
Engaging new story explores fear and hope, faith and gratitude in ways that will delight kids and adults—inspiring us to bless each of God's days and nights.
9 x 12, 32 pp, Full-color illus., Hardcover, ISBN 1-58023-177-2 **$17.95** *For ages 4 & up*

But God Remembered
Stories of Women from Creation to the Promised Land
Four different stories of women—Lillith, Serach, Bityah, and the Daughters of Z—teach us important values through their faith and actions.
9 x 12, 32 pp, Full-color illus., Hardcover, ISBN 1-879045-43-5 **$16.95** *For ages 8 & up*

Cain & Abel: Finding the Fruits of Peace
Shows children that we have the power to deal with anger in positive ways. Provides questions for kids and adults to explore together.
9 x 12, 32 pp, Full-color illus., Hardcover, ISBN 1-58023-123-3 **$16.95** *For ages 5 & up*

God in Between
If you wanted to find God, where would you look? This magical, mythical tale teaches that God can be found where we are: within all of us and the relationships between us.
9 x 12, 32 pp, Full-color illus., Hardcover, ISBN 1-879045-86-9 **$16.95** *For ages 4 & up*

God's Paintbrush: Special 10th Anniversary Edition
Wonderfully interactive, invites children of all faiths and backgrounds to encounter God through moments in their own lives. Provides questions adult and child can explore together.
11 x 8½, 32 pp, Full-color illus., Hardcover, ISBN 1-58023-195-0 **$17.95** *For ages 4 & up*

Also Available: **God's Paintbrush Teacher's Guide**
8½ x 11, 32 pp, PB, ISBN 1-879045-57-5 **$8.95**

God's Paintbrush Celebration Kit
A Spiritual Activity Kit for Teachers and Students of All Faiths, All Backgrounds
Additional activity sheets available:
8-Student Activity Sheet Pack (40 sheets/5 sessions), ISBN 1-58023-058-X **$19.95**
Single-Student Activity Sheet Pack (5 sessions), ISBN 1-58023-059-8 **$3.95**

In God's Name
Like an ancient myth in its poetic text and vibrant illustrations, this award-winning modern fable about the search for God's name celebrates the diversity and, at the same time, the unity of all people.
9 x 12, 32 pp, Full-color illus., Hardcover, ISBN 1-879045-26-5 **$16.99** *For ages 4 & up*

Also Available as a Board Book: **What Is God's Name?**
5 x 5, 24 pp, Board, Full-color illus., ISBN 1-893361-10-1 **$7.99** *For ages 0–4 (A SkyLight Paths book)*

Also Available: **In God's Name video and study guide**
Computer animation, original music, and children's voices. 18 min. **$29.99**

Also Available in Spanish: **El nombre de Dios**
9 x 12, 32 pp, Full-color illus., Hardcover, ISBN 1-893361-63-2 **$16.95** *(A SkyLight Paths book)*

Noah's Wife: The Story of Naamah
When God tells Noah to bring the animals of the world onto the ark, God also calls on Naamah, Noah's wife, to save each plant on Earth. Based on an ancient text.
9 x 12, 32 pp, Full-color illus., Hardcover, ISBN 1-58023-134-9 **$16.95** *For ages 4 & up*

Also Available as a Board Book: **Naamah, Noah's Wife**
5 x 5, 24 pp, Full-color illus., Board, ISBN 1-893361-56-X **$7.95** *For ages 0–4 (A SkyLight Paths book)*

For Heaven's Sake: Finding God in Unexpected Places
9 x 12, 32 pp, Full-color illus., Hardcover, ISBN 1-58023-054-7 **$16.95** *For ages 4 & up*

God Said Amen: Finding the Answers to Our Prayers
9 x 12, 32 pp, Full-color illus., Hardcover, ISBN 1-58023-080-6 **$16.95** *For ages 4 & up*

Current Events/History

The Story of the Jews: A 4,000-Year Adventure—A Graphic History Book
Written & illustrated by Stan Mack
Witty, illustrated narrative of all the major happenings from biblical times to the
twenty-first century.   6 x 9, 288 pp, illus., Quality PB, ISBN 1-58023-155-1 **$16.95**

Hannah Senesh: Her Life and Diary, the First Complete Edition
By Hannah Senesh; Foreword by Marge Piercy; Preface by Eitan Senesh
6 x 9, 352 pp, Hardcover, ISBN 1-58023-212-4 **$24.99**

The Jewish Prophet: Visionary Words from Moses and Miriam to Henrietta Szold
and A. J. Heschel   *By Rabbi Michael J. Shire*
6½ x 8½, 128 pp, 123 full-color illus., Hardcover, ISBN 1-58023-168-3 **Special gift price $14.95**

Shared Dreams: Martin Luther King, Jr. & the Jewish Community
By Rabbi Marc Schneier. Preface by Martin Luther King III.
6 x 9, 240 pp, Hardcover, ISBN 1-58023-062-8 **$24.95**

"Who Is a Jew?": Conversations, Not Conclusions *By Meryl Hyman*
6 x 9, 272 pp, Quality PB, ISBN 1-58023-052-0 **$16.95**

Ecology

Ecology & the Jewish Spirit: Where Nature & the Sacred Meet
Edited by Ellen Bernstein 6 x 9, 288 pp, Quality PB, ISBN 1-58023-082-2 **$16.95**

Torah of the Earth: Exploring 4,000 Years of Ecology in Jewish Thought
Vol. 1: Biblical Israel: One Land, One People; Rabbinic Judaism: One People, Many Lands
Vol. 2: Zionism: One Land, Two Peoples; Eco-Judaism: One Earth, Many Peoples
Edited by Rabbi Arthur Waskow
Vol. 1: 6 x 9, 272 pp, Quality PB, ISBN 1-58023-086-5 **$19.95**
Vol. 2: 6 x 9, 336 pp, Quality PB, ISBN 1-58023-087-3 **$19.95**

The Way Into Judaism and the Environment
By Jeremy Benstein, PhD
6 x 9, 225 pp (est.), Hardcover, ISBN 1-58023-268-X **$24.99**

Grief/Healing

Against the Dying of the Light: A Parent's Story of Love, Loss and Hope
By Leonard Fein
5½ x 8½, 176 pp, Quality PB, ISBN 1-58023-197-7 **$15.99;** Hardcover, ISBN 1-58023-110-1 **$19.95**

Grief in Our Seasons: A Mourner's Kaddish Companion *By Rabbi Kerry M. Olitzky*
4½ x 6¼, 448 pp, Quality PB, ISBN 1-879045-55-9 **$15.95**

Healing of Soul, Healing of Body: Spiritual Leaders Unfold the Strength & Solace
in Psalms *Edited by Rabbi Simkha Y. Weintraub, C.S.W.*
6 x 9, 128 pp, 2-color illus. text, Quality PB, ISBN 1-879045-31-1 **$14.99**

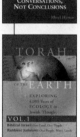

Jewish Paths toward Healing and Wholeness: A Personal Guide to Dealing with
Suffering *By Rabbi Kerry M. Olitzky. Foreword by Debbie Friedman.*
6 x 9, 192 pp, Quality PB, ISBN 1-58023-068-7 **$15.95**

Mourning & Mitzvah, 2nd Edition: A Guided Journal for Walking the Mourner's
Path through Grief to Healing *By Anne Brener, L.C.S.W.*
7½ x 9, 304 pp, Quality PB, ISBN 1-58023-113-6 **$19.95**

The Perfect Stranger's Guide to Funerals and Grieving Practices
A Guide to Etiquette in Other People's Religious Ceremonies *Edited by Stuart M. Matlins*
6 x 9, 240 pp, Quality PB, ISBN 1-893361-20-9 **$16.95** *(A SkyLight Paths book)*

Tears of Sorrow, Seeds of Hope: A Jewish Spiritual Companion for Infertility and
Pregnancy Loss *By Rabbi Nina Beth Cardin*
6 x 9, 192 pp, Hardcover, ISBN 1-58023-017-2 **$19.95**

A Time to Mourn, A Time to Comfort, 2nd Edition: A Guide to Jewish
Bereavement and Comfort *By Dr. Ron Wolfson*
7 x 9, 336 pp, Quality PB, ISBN 1-58023-253-1 **$19.99**

When a Grandparent Dies: A Kid's Own Remembering Workbook for Dealing
with Shiva and the Year Beyond *By Nechama Liss-Levinson, Ph.D.*
8 x 10, 48 pp, 2-color text, Hardcover, ISBN 1-879045-44-3 **$15.95** *For ages 7–13*

Life Cycle
Marriage / Parenting / Family / Aging

Jewish Fathers: A Legacy of Love
Photographs by Lloyd Wolf. Essays by Paula Wolfson. Foreword by Harold S. Kushner.
Honors the role of contemporary Jewish fathers in America. Each father tells in his own words what it means to be a parent and Jewish, and what he learned from his own father. Insightful photos. 9½ x 9⅞, 144 pp with 100+ duotone photos, Hardcover, ISBN 1-58023-204-3 **$30.00**

The New Jewish Baby Album: Creating and Celebrating the Beginning of a Spiritual Life—A Jewish Lights Companion
By the Editors at Jewish Lights. Foreword by Anita Diamant. Preface by Sandy Eisenberg Sasso.
A spiritual keepsake that will be treasured for generations. More than just a memory book, *shows you how—and why it's important*—to create a Jewish home and a Jewish life. 8 x 10, 64 pp, Deluxe Padded Hardcover, Full-color illus., ISBN 1-58023-138-1 **$19.95**

The Jewish Pregnancy Book: A Resource for the Soul, Body & Mind during Pregnancy, Birth & the First Three Months
By Sandy Falk, M.D., and Rabbi Daniel Judson, with Steven A. Rapp
Includes medical information, prayers and rituals for each stage of pregnancy, from a liberal Jewish perspective. 7 x 10, 208 pp, Quality PB, b/w illus., ISBN 1-58023-178-0 **$16.95**

Celebrating Your New Jewish Daughter: Creating Jewish Ways to Welcome Baby Girls into the Covenant—New and Traditional Ceremonies
By Debra Nussbaum Cohen 6 x 9, 272 pp, Quality PB, ISBN 1-58023-090-3 **$18.95**

The New Jewish Baby Book, 2nd Edition: Names, Ceremonies & Customs—A Guide for Today's Families *By Anita Diamant* 6 x 9, 336 pp, Quality PB, ISBN 1-58023-251-5 **$19.99**

Parenting As a Spiritual Journey: Deepening Ordinary and Extraordinary Events into Sacred Occasions *By Rabbi Nancy Fuchs-Kreimer* 6 x 9, 224 pp, Quality PB, ISBN 1-58023-016-4 **$16.95**

Judaism for Two: A Spiritual Guide for Strengthening and Celebrating Your Loving Relationship *By Rabbi Nancy Fuchs-Kreimer and Rabbi Nancy H. Wiener*
Addresses the ways Jewish teachings can enhance and strengthen committed relationships. 6 x 9, 208 pp, Quality PB, ISBN 1-58023-254-X **$16.99**

Embracing the Covenant: Converts to Judaism Talk About Why & How
By Rabbi Allan Berkowitz and Patti Moskovitz 6 x 9, 192 pp, Quality PB, ISBN 1-879045-50-8 **$16.95**

The Guide to Jewish Interfaith Family Life: An InterfaithFamily.com Handbook
Edited by Ronnie Friedland and Edmund Case 6 x 9, 384 pp, Quality PB, ISBN 1-58023-153-5 **$18.95**

Introducing My Faith and My Community
The Jewish Outreach Institute Guide for the Christian in a Jewish Interfaith Relationship
By Rabbi Kerry M. Olitzky 6 x 9, 176 pp, Quality PB, ISBN 1-58023-192-6 **$16.99**

Making a Successful Jewish Interfaith Marriage: The Jewish Outreach Institute Guide to Opportunities, Challenges and Resources
By Rabbi Kerry M. Olitzky with Joan Peterson Littman 6 x 9, 176 pp, Quality PB, ISBN 1-58023-170-5 **$16.95**

The Creative Jewish Wedding Book: A Hands-On Guide to New & Old Traditions, Ceremonies & Celebrations *By Gabrielle Kaplan-Mayer*
Provides the tools to create the most meaningful Jewish traditional or alternative wedding by using ritual elements to express your unique style and spirituality. 9 x 9, 288 pp, b/w photos, Quality PB, ISBN 1-58023-194-2 **$19.99**

Divorce Is a Mitzvah: A Practical Guide to Finding Wholeness and Holiness When Your Marriage Dies *By Rabbi Perry Netter. Afterword by Rabbi Laura Geller.*
6 x 9, 224 pp, Quality PB, ISBN 1-58023-172-1 **$16.95**

A Heart of Wisdom: Making the Jewish Journey from Midlife through the Elder Years
Edited by Susan Berrin. Foreword by Harold Kushner. 6 x 9, 384 pp, Quality PB, ISBN 1-58023-051-2 **$18.95**

So That Your Values Live On: Ethical Wills and How to Prepare Them
Edited by Jack Riemer and Nathaniel Stampfer 6 x 9, 272 pp, Quality PB, ISBN 1-879045-34-6 **$18.95**

Holidays/Holy Days

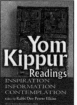

Yom Kippur Readings: Inspiration, Information and Contemplation
Edited by Rabbi Dov Peretz Elkins with section introductions from Arthur Green's These Are the Words
An extraordinary collection of readings, prayers and insights that enable the modern worshiper to enter into the spirit of the Day of Atonement in a personal and powerful way, permitting the meaning of Yom Kippur to enter the heart.
6 x 9, 348 pp, Hardcover, ISBN 1-58023-271-X **$24.99**

Leading the Passover Journey
The Seder's Meaning Revealed, the Haggadah's Story Retold
By Rabbi Nathan Laufer
Uncovers the hidden meaning of the Seder's rituals and customs
6 x 9, 208 pp, Hardcover, ISBN 1-58023-211-6 **$24.99**

Reclaiming Judaism as a Spiritual Practice: Holy Days and Shabbat
By Rabbi Goldie Milgram
Provides a framework for understanding the powerful and often unexplained intellectual, emotional, and spiritual tools that are essential for a lively, relevant, and fulfilling Jewish spiritual practice. 7 x 9, 272 pp, Quality PB, ISBN 1-58023-205-1 **$19.99**

7th Heaven: Celebrating Shabbat with Rebbe Nachman of Breslov
By Moshe Mykoff with the Breslov Research Institute
Explores the art of consciously observing Shabbat and understanding in-depth many of the day's spiritual practices. 5⅛ x 8¼, 224 pp, Deluxe PB w/flaps, ISBN 1-58023-175-6 **$18.95**

The Women's Passover Companion
Women's Reflections on the Festival of Freedom
Edited by Rabbi Sharon Cohen Anisfeld, Tara Mohr, and Catherine Spector
Groundbreaking. A provocative conversation about women's relationships to Passover as well as the roots and meanings of women's seders.
6 x 9, 352 pp, Quality PB, ISBN 1-58023-231-0 **$19.99**; Hardcover, ISBN 1-58023-128-4 **$24.95**

The Women's Seder Sourcebook
Rituals & Readings for Use at the Passover Seder
Edited by Rabbi Sharon Cohen Anisfeld, Tara Mohr, and Catherine Spector
Gathers the voices of more than one hundred women in readings, personal and creative reflections, commentaries, blessings, and ritual suggestions that can be incorporated into your Passover celebration.
6 x 9, 384 pp, Quality PB, ISBN 1-58023-232-9 **$19.99**; Hardcover, ISBN 1-58023-136-5 **$24.95**

Creating Lively Passover Seders: A Sourcebook of Engaging Tales, Texts & Activities
By David Arnow, Ph.D. 7 x 9, 416 pp, Quality PB, ISBN 1-58023-184-5 **$24.99**

Hanukkah, 2nd Edition: The Family Guide to Spiritual Celebration
By Dr. Ron Wolfson. Edited by Joel Lurie Grishaver.
7 x 9, 240 pp, illus., Quality PB, ISBN 1-58023-122-5 **$18.95**

The Jewish Family Fun Book: Holiday Projects, Everyday Activities, and Travel Ideas with Jewish Themes *By Danielle Dardashti and Roni Sarig. Illus. by Avi Katz.*
6 x 9, 288 pp, 70+ b/w illus. & diagrams, Quality PB, ISBN 1-58023-171-3 **$18.95**

The Jewish Gardening Cookbook: Growing Plants & Cooking for Holidays & Festivals *By Michael Brown* 6 x 9, 224 pp, 30+ illus., Quality PB, ISBN 1-58023-116-0 **$16.95**

The Jewish Lights Book of Fun Classroom Activities: Simple and Seasonal Projects for Teachers and Students *By Danielle Dardashti and Roni Sarig*
6 x 9, 240 pp, Quality PB, ISBN 1–58023–206–X **$19.99**

Passover, 2nd Edition: The Family Guide to Spiritual Celebration
By Dr. Ron Wolfson with Joel Lurie Grishaver 7 x 9, 352 pp, Quality PB, ISBN 1-58023-174-8 **$19.95**

Shabbat, 2nd Edition: The Family Guide to Preparing for and Celebrating the Sabbath
By Dr. Ron Wolfson 7 x 9, 320 pp, illus., Quality PB, ISBN 1-58023-164-0 **$19.95**

Sharing Blessings: Children's Stories for Exploring the Spirit of the Jewish Holidays
By Rahel Musleah and Michael Klayman
8½ x 11, 64 pp, Full-color illus., Hardcover, ISBN 1-879045-71-0 **$18.95** *For ages 6 & up*

Theology/Philosophy

Aspects of Rabbinic Theology
By Solomon Schechter. New Introduction by Dr. Neil Gillman.
6 x 9, 448 pp, Quality PB, ISBN 1-879045-24-9 **$19.95**

Broken Tablets: Restoring the Ten Commandments and Ourselves
Edited by Rachel S. Mikva. Introduction by Lawrence Kushner. Afterword by Arnold Jacob Wolf.
6 x 9, 192 pp, Quality PB, ISBN 1-58023-158-6 **$16.95**; Hardcover, ISBN 1-58023-066-0 **$21.95**

Creating an Ethical Jewish Life
A Practical Introduction to Classic Teachings on How to Be a Jew
By Dr. Byron L. Sherwin and Seymour J. Cohen
6 x 9, 336 pp, Quality PB, ISBN 1-58023-114-4 **$19.95**

The Death of Death: Resurrection and Immortality in Jewish Thought
By Dr. Neil Gillman 6 x 9, 336 pp, Quality PB, ISBN 1-58023-081-4 **$18.95**

Evolving Halakhah: A Progressive Approach to Traditional Jewish Law
By Rabbi Dr. Moshe Zemer
6 x 9, 480 pp, Quality PB, ISBN 1-58023-127-6 **$29.95**; Hardcover, ISBN 1-58023-002-4 **$40.00**

Hasidic Tales: Annotated & Explained
By Rabbi Rami Shapiro. Foreword by Andrew Harvey, SkyLight Illuminations series editor.
5½ x 8½, 240 pp, Quality PB, ISBN 1-893361-86-1 **$16.95** *(A SkyLight Paths Book)*

A Heart of Many Rooms: Celebrating the Many Voices within Judaism
By Dr. David Hartman 6 x 9, 352 pp, Quality PB, ISBN 1-58023-156-X **$19.95**

The Hebrew Prophets: Selections Annotated & Explained
Translation & Annotation by Rabbi Rami Shapiro. Foreword by Zalman M. Schachter-Shalomi
5½ x 8½, 224 pp, Quality PB, ISBN 1-59473-037-7 **$16.99** *(A SkyLight Paths book)*

Keeping Faith with the Psalms: Deepen Your Relationship with God Using the
Book of Psalms *By Daniel F. Polish* 6 x 9, 320 pp, Quality PB, ISBN 1-58023-300-7 **$18.99**;
Hardcover, ISBN 1-58023-179-9 **$24.95**

The Last Trial
On the Legends and Lore of the Command to Abraham to Offer Isaac as a Sacrifice
By Shalom Spiegel. New Introduction by Judah Goldin.
6 x 9, 208 pp, Quality PB, ISBN 1-879045-29-X **$18.95**

A Living Covenant: The Innovative Spirit in Traditional Judaism
By Dr. David Hartman 6 x 9, 368 pp, Quality PB, ISBN 1-58023-011-3 **$18.95**

Love and Terror in the God Encounter
The Theological Legacy of Rabbi Joseph B. Soloveitchik
By Dr. David Hartman
6 x 9, 240 pp, Quality PB, ISBN 1-58023-176-4 **$19.95**; Hardcover, ISBN 1-58023-112-8 **$25.00**

The Personhood of God: Biblical Theology, Human Faith and the Divine Image
By Dr. Yochanan Muffs; Foreword by Dr. David Hartman
6 x 9, 240 pp, Hardcover, ISBN 1-58023-265-5 **$24.99**

The Spirit of Renewal: Finding Faith after the Holocaust
By Rabbi Edward Feld 6 x 9, 224 pp, Quality PB, ISBN 1-879045-40-0 **$16.95**

Tormented Master: *The Life and Spiritual Quest of Rabbi Nahman of Bratslav*
By Dr. Arthur Green 6 x 9, 416 pp, Quality PB, ISBN 1-879045-11-7 **$19.99**

Your Word Is Fire: The Hasidic Masters on Contemplative Prayer
Edited and translated by Dr. Arthur Green and Barry W. Holtz
6 x 9, 160 pp, Quality PB, ISBN 1-879045-25-7 **$15.95**

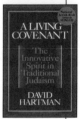
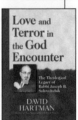

I Am Jewish
Personal Reflections Inspired by the Last Words of Daniel Pearl
Almost 150 Jews—both famous and not—from all walks of life, from all around
the world, write about Identity, Heritage, Covenant / Chosenness and Faith,
Humanity and Ethnicity, and *Tikkun Olam* and Justice.
Edited by Judea and Ruth Pearl
6 x 9, 304 pp, Deluxe PB w/flaps, ISBN 1-58023-259-0 **$18.99**; Hardcover, ISBN 1-58023-183-7 **$24.99**
Download a free copy of the *I Am Jewish Teacher's Guide* at our website:
www.jewishlights.com

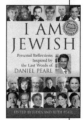

Spirituality

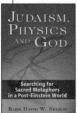

Does the Soul Survive? A Jewish Journey to Belief in Afterlife, Past Lives & Living with Purpose   *By Rabbi Elie Kaplan Spitz. Foreword by Brian L. Weiss, M.D.*
Spitz relates his own experiences and those shared with him by people he has worked with as a rabbi, and shows us that belief in afterlife and past lives, so often approached with reluctance, is in fact true to Jewish tradition.
6 x 9, 288 pp, Quality PB, ISBN 1-58023-165-9 **$16.95**; Hardcover, ISBN 1-58023-094-6 **$21.95**

First Steps to a New Jewish Spirit: Reb Zalman's Guide to Recapturing the Intimacy & Ecstasy in Your Relationship with God
By Rabbi Zalman M. Schachter-Shalomi with Donald Gropman
An extraordinary spiritual handbook that restores psychic and physical vigor by introducing us to new models and alternative ways of practicing Judaism. Offers meditation and contemplation exercises for enriching the most important aspects of everyday life.   6 x 9, 144 pp, Quality PB, ISBN 1-58023-182-9 **$16.95**

God in Our Relationships: Spirituality between People from the Teachings of Martin Buber   *By Rabbi Dennis S. Ross*
On the eightieth anniversary of Buber's classic work, we can discover new answers to critical issues in our lives. Inspiring examples from Ross's own life— as congregational rabbi, father, hospital chaplain, social worker, and husband— illustrate Buber's difficult-to-understand ideas about how we encounter God and each other. 5½ x 8½, 160 pp, Quality PB, ISBN 1-58023-147-0 **$16.95**

Judaism, Physics and God: Searching for Sacred Metaphors in a Post-Einstein World   *By Rabbi David W. Nelson*
In clear, non-technical terms, this provocative fusion of religion and science examines the great theories of modern physics to find new ways for contemporary people to express their spiritual beliefs and thoughts.
6 x 9, 352 pp, Hardcover, ISBN 1-58023-252-3 **$24.99**

The Jewish Lights Spirituality Handbook: A Guide to Understanding, Exploring & Living a Spiritual Life   *Edited by Stuart M. Matlins*
What exactly is "Jewish" about spirituality? How do I make it a part of my life? Fifty of today's foremost spiritual leaders share their ideas and experience with us.
6 x 9, 456 pp, Quality PB, ISBN 1-58023-093-8 **$19.95**; Hardcover, ISBN 1-58023-100-4 **$24.95**

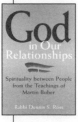

Bringing the Psalms to Life: How to Understand and Use the Book of Psalms
By Dr. Daniel F. Polish
6 x 9, 208 pp, Quality PB, ISBN 1-58023-157-8 **$16.95**; Hardcover, ISBN 1-58023-077-6 **$21.95**

God & the Big Bang: Discovering Harmony between Science & Spirituality
By Dr. Daniel C. Matt 6 x 9, 216 pp, Quality PB, ISBN 1-879045-89-3 **$16.95**

Godwrestling—Round 2: Ancient Wisdom, Future Paths
By Rabbi Arthur Waskow 6 x 9, 352 pp, Quality PB, ISBN 1-879045-72-9 **$18.95**

One God Clapping: The Spiritual Path of a Zen Rabbi   *By Rabbi Alan Lew with Sherril Jaffe*
5½ x 8½, 336 pp, Quality PB, ISBN 1-58023-115-2 **$16.95**

The Path of Blessing: Experiencing the Energy and Abundance of the Divine
By Rabbi Marcia Prager 5½ x 8½, 240 pp., Quality PB, ISBN 1-58023-148-9 **$16.95**

Six Jewish Spiritual Paths: A Rationalist Looks at Spirituality   *By Rabbi Rifat Sonsino*
6 x 9, 208 pp, Quality PB, ISBN 1-58023-167-5 **$16.95**; Hardcover, ISBN 1-58023-095-4 **$21.95**

Soul Judaism: Dancing with God into a New Era
By Rabbi Wayne Dosick 5½ x 8½, 304 pp, Quality PB, ISBN 1-58023-053-9 **$16.95**

Stepping Stones to Jewish Spiritual Living: Walking the Path Morning, Noon, and Night   *By Rabbi James L. Mirel and Karen Bonnell Werth*
6 x 9, 240 pp, Quality PB, ISBN 1-58023-074-1 **$16.95**; Hardcover, ISBN 1-58023-003-2 **$21.95**

There Is No Messiah ... and You're It: The Stunning Transformation of Judaism's Most Provocative Idea   *By Rabbi Robert N. Levine, D.D.*
6 x 9, 192 pp, Quality PB, ISBN 1-58023-255-8 **$16.99**; Hardcover, ISBN 1-58023-173-X **$21.95**

These Are the Words: A Vocabulary of Jewish Spiritual Life   *By Dr. Arthur Green*
6 x 9, 304 pp, Quality PB, ISBN 1-58023-107-1 **$18.95**

Meditation

The Handbook of Jewish Meditation Practices
A Guide for Enriching the Sabbath and Other Days of Your Life
By Rabbi David A. Cooper
Easy-to-learn meditation techniques. 6 x 9, 208 pp, Quality PB, ISBN 1-58023-102-0 **$16.95**

Discovering Jewish Meditation: Instruction & Guidance for Learning an Ancient
Spiritual Practice *By Nan Fink Gefen, Ph.D.* 6 x 9, 208 pp, Quality PB, ISBN 1-58023-067-9 **$16.95**

A Heart of Stillness: A Complete Guide to Learning the Art of Meditation
By Rabbi David A. Cooper 5½ x 8½, 272 pp, Quality PB, ISBN 1-893361-03-9 **$16.95**
(A SkyLight Paths book)

Meditation from the Heart of Judaism: Today's Teachers Share Their
Practices, Techniques, and Faith *Edited by Avram Davis*
6 x 9, 256 pp, Quality PB, ISBN 1-58023-049-0 **$16.95**

Silence, Simplicity & Solitude: A Complete Guide to Spiritual Retreat at Home
By Rabbi David A. Cooper 5½ x 8½, 336 pp, Quality PB, ISBN 1-893361-04-7 **$16.95**
(A SkyLight Paths book)

The Way of Flame: A Guide to the Forgotten Mystical Tradition of Jewish
Meditation *By Avram Davis* 4½ x 8, 176 pp, Quality PB, ISBN 1-58023-060-1 **$15.95**

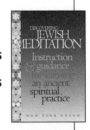

Ritual/Sacred Practice/Journaling

The Jewish Dream Book: The Key to Opening the Inner Meaning of
Your Dreams *By Vanessa L. Ochs with Elizabeth Ochs; Full-color illus. by Kristina Swarner*
Instructions for how modern people can perform ancient Jewish dream practices
and dream interpretations drawn from the Jewish wisdom tradition. For anyone
who wants to understand their dreams—and themselves.
8 x 8, 120 pp, Full-color illus., Deluxe PB w/flaps, ISBN 1-58023-132-2 **$16.95**

The Jewish Journaling Book: How to Use Jewish Tradition to Write
Your Life & Explore Your Soul *By Janet Ruth Falon*
Details the history of Jewish journaling throughout biblical and modern times,
and teaches specific journaling techniques to help you create and maintain a vital
journal, from a Jewish perspective. 8 x 8, 304 pp, Deluxe PB w/flaps, ISBN 1-58023-203-5 **$18.99**

The Book of Jewish Sacred Practices: CLAL's Guide to Everyday & Holiday
Rituals & Blessings *Edited by Rabbi Irwin Kula and Vanessa L. Ochs, Ph.D.*
6 x 9, 368 pp, Quality PB, ISBN 1-58023-152-7 **$18.95**

Jewish Ritual: A Brief Introduction for Christians
By Rabbi Kerry M. Olitzky and Rabbi Daniel Judson
5½ x 8½, 144 pp, Quality PB, ISBN 1-58023-210-8 **$14.99**

The Rituals & Practices of a Jewish Life: A Handbook for Personal Spiritual
Renewal *Edited by Rabbi Kerry M. Olitzky and Rabbi Daniel Judson*
6 x 9, 272 pp, illus., Quality PB, ISBN 1-58023-169-1 **$18.95**

Science Fiction/
Mystery & Detective Fiction

Mystery Midrash: An Anthology of Jewish Mystery & Detective Fiction
Edited by Lawrence W. Raphael. Preface by Joel Siegel.
6 x 9, 304 pp, Quality PB, ISBN 1-58023-055-5 **$16.95**

Criminal Kabbalah: An Intriguing Anthology of Jewish Mystery & Detective Fiction
Edited by Lawrence W. Raphael. Foreword by Laurie R. King.
6 x 9, 256 pp, Quality PB, ISBN 1-58023-109-8 **$16.95**

Wandering Stars: An Anthology of Jewish Fantasy & Science Fiction
Edited by Jack Dann. Introduction by Isaac Asimov.
6 x 9, 272 pp, Quality PB, ISBN 1-58023-005-9 **$16.95**

More Wandering Stars: An Anthology of Outstanding Stories of Jewish Fantasy and
Science Fiction *Edited by Jack Dann. Introduction by Isaac Asimov.*
6 x 9, 192 pp, Quality PB, ISBN 1-58023-063-6 **$16.95**

Spirituality/Women's Interest

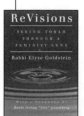

The Quotable Jewish Woman: Wisdom, Inspiration & Humor from the Mind & Heart *Edited and compiled by Elaine Bernstein Partnow*
The definitive collection of ideas, reflections, humor, and wit of over 300 Jewish women.
6 x 9, 496 pp, Hardcover, ISBN 1-58023-193-4 **$29.99**

Lifecycles, Vol. 1: Jewish Women on Life Passages & Personal Milestones
Edited and with introductions by Rabbi Debra Orenstein 6 x 9, 480 pp, Quality PB, ISBN 1-58023-018-0 **$19.95**

Lifecycles, Vol. 2: Jewish Women on Biblical Themes in Contemporary Life
Edited and with introductions by Rabbi Debra Orenstein and Rabbi Jane Rachel Litman
6 x 9, 464 pp, Quality PB, ISBN 1-58023-019-9 **$19.95**

Moonbeams: A Hadassah Rosh Hodesh Guide *Edited by Carol Diament, Ph.D.*
8½ x 11, 240 pp, Quality PB, ISBN 1-58023-099-7 **$20.00**

ReVisions: Seeing Torah through a Feminist Lens *By Rabbi Elyse Goldstein*
5½ x 8½, 224 pp, Quality PB, ISBN 1-58023-117-9 **$16.95**

White Fire: A Portrait of Women Spiritual Leaders in America
By Rabbi Malka Drucker. Photographs by Gay Block.
7 x 10, 320 pp, 30+ b/w photos, Hardcover, ISBN 1-893361-64-0 **$24.95** *(A SkyLight Paths book)*

Women of the Wall: Claiming Sacred Ground at Judaism's Holy Site
Edited by Phyllis Chesler and Rivka Haut 6 x 9, 496 pp, b/w photos, Hardcover, ISBN 1-58023-161-6 **$34.95**

The Women's Haftarah Commentary: New Insights from Women Rabbis on the 54 Weekly Haftarah Portions, the 5 Megillot & Special Shabbatot
Edited by Rabbi Elyse Goldstein 6 x 9, 560 pp, Hardcover, ISBN 1-58023-133-0 **$39.99**

The Women's Torah Commentary: New Insights from Women Rabbis on the 54 Weekly Torah Portions *Edited by Rabbi Elyse Goldstein*
6 x 9, 496 pp, Hardcover, ISBN 1-58023-076-8 **$34.95**

The Year Mom Got Religion: One Woman's Midlife Journey into Judaism
By Lee Meyerhoff Hendler 6 x 9, 208 pp, Quality PB, ISBN 1-58023-070-9 **$15.95**

See Holidays for *The Women's Passover Companion: Women's Reflections on the Festival of Freedom* and *The Women's Seder Sourcebook: Rituals & Readings for Use at the Passover Seder.* Also see Bar/Bat Mitzvah for *The JGirl's Guide: The Young Jewish Woman's Handbook for Coming of Age.*

Travel

Israel—A Spiritual Travel Guide, 2nd Edition
A Companion for the Modern Jewish Pilgrim
By Rabbi Lawrence A. Hoffman 4¾ x 10, 256 pp, Quality PB, illus., ISBN 1-58023-261-2 **$18.99**
Also Available: **The Israel Mission Leader's Guide** ISBN 1-58023-085-7 **$4.95**

12 Steps

100 Blessings Every Day Daily Twelve Step Recovery Affirmations, Exercises for Personal Growth & Renewal Reflecting Seasons of the Jewish Year
By Rabbi Kerry M. Olitzky. Foreword by Rabbi Neil Gillman.
One-day-at-a-time monthly format. Reflects on the rhythm of the Jewish calendar to bring insight to recovery from addictions.
4½ x 6½, 432 pp, Quality PB, ISBN 1-879045-30-3 **$15.99**

Recovery from Codependence: A Jewish Twelve Steps Guide to Healing Your Soul
By Rabbi Kerry M. Olitzky 6 x 9, 160 pp, Quality PB, ISBN 1-879045-32-X **$13.95**

Renewed Each Day: Daily Twelve Step Recovery Meditations Based on the Bible
By Rabbi Kerry M. Olitzky and Aaron Z.
Vol. 1—Genesis & Exodus: 6 x 9, 224 pp, Quality PB, ISBN 1-879045-12-5 **$14.95**
Vol. 2—Leviticus, Numbers & Deuteronomy: 6 x 9, 280 pp, Quality PB, ISBN 1-879045-13-3 **$18.99**

Twelve Jewish Steps to Recovery: A Personal Guide to Turning from Alcoholism & Other Addictions—Drugs, Food, Gambling, Sex...
By Rabbi Kerry M. Olitzky and Stuart A. Copans, M.D. Preface by Abraham J. Twerski, M.D.
6 x 9, 144 pp, Quality PB, ISBN 1-879045-09-5 **$14.95**

Spirituality/The Way Into... Series

The Way Into... Series offers an accessible and highly usable "guided tour" of the Jewish faith, people, history and beliefs—in total, an introduction to Judaism that will enable you to understand and interact with the sacred texts of the Jewish tradition. Each volume is written by a leading contemporary scholar and teacher, and explores one key aspect of Judaism. *The Way Into...* enables all readers to achieve a real sense of Jewish cultural literacy through guided study.

The Way Into Encountering God in Judaism   *By Neil Gillman*
6 x 9, 240 pp, Quality PB, ISBN 1-58023-199-3 **$18.99**; Hardcover, ISBN 1-58023-025-3 **$21.95**
Also Available: **The Jewish Approach to God: A Brief Introduction for Christians**
By Neil Gillman 5½ x 8½, 192 pp, Quality PB, ISBN 1-58023-190-X **$16.95**

The Way Into Jewish Mystical Tradition   *By Lawrence Kushner*
6 x 9, 224 pp, Quality PB, ISBN 1-58023-200-0 **$18.99**; Hardcover, ISBN 1-58023-029-6 **$21.95**

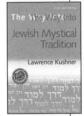

The Way Into Jewish Prayer   *By Lawrence A. Hoffman*
6 x 9, 224 pp, Quality PB, ISBN 1-58023-201-9 **$18.99**; Hardcover, ISBN 1-58023-027-X **$21.95**

The Way Into the Relationship between Jews and Non-Jews: Searching for Boundaries and Bridges   *By Michael A. Signer, PhD*
6 x 9, 225 pp (est.), Hardcover, ISBN 1-58023-267-1 **$24.99**

The Way Into Judaism and the Environment   *By Jeremy Benstein, PhD*
6 x 9, 225 pp (est.), Hardcover, ISBN 1-58023-268-X **$24.99**

The Way Into *Tikkun Olam* (Repairing the World)   *By Elliot N. Dorff*
6 x 9, 320 pp, Hardcover, ISBN 1-58023-269-8 **$24.99**

The Way Into Torah   *By Norman J. Cohen*
6 x 9, 176 pp, Quality PB, ISBN 1-58023-198-5 **$16.99**; Hardcover, ISBN 1-58023-028-8 **$21.95**

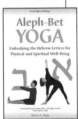

Spirituality and Wellness

Aleph-Bet Yoga
Embodying the Hebrew Letters for Physical and Spiritual Well-Being
By Steven A. Rapp. Foreword by Tamar Frankiel, Ph.D., and Judy Greenfeld. Preface by Hart Lazer
7 x 10, 128 pp, b/w photos, Quality PB, Layflat binding, ISBN 1-58023-162-4 **$16.95**

Entering the Temple of Dreams
Jewish Prayers, Movements, and Meditations for the End of the Day
By Tamar Frankiel, Ph.D., and Judy Greenfeld
7 x 10, 192 pp, illus., Quality PB, ISBN 1-58023-079-2 **$16.95**

Jewish Paths toward Healing and Wholeness: A Personal Guide to Dealing with Suffering   *By Rabbi Kerry M. Olitzky. Foreword by Debbie Friedman.*
6 x 9, 192 pp, Quality PB, ISBN 1-58023-068-7 **$15.95**

Minding the Temple of the Soul
Balancing Body, Mind, and Spirit through Traditional Jewish Prayer, Movement, and Meditation   *By Tamar Frankiel, Ph.D., and Judy Greenfeld*
7 x 10, 184 pp, illus., Quality PB, ISBN 1-879045-64-8 **$16.95**
Audiotape of the Blessings and Meditations: 60 min. **$9.95**
Videotape of the Movements and Meditations: 46 min. **$20.00**

Inspiration

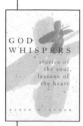

God in All Moments
Mystical & Practical Spiritual Wisdom from Hasidic Masters
Edited and translated by Or N. Rose with Ebn D. Leader
Hasidic teachings on how to be mindful in religious practice and cultivating every-day ethical behavior—*hanhagot*. 5½ x 8½, 192 pp, Quality PB, ISBN 1-58023-186-1 **$16.95**

Our Dance with God: Finding Prayer, Perspective and Meaning in the Stories of Our Lives *By Karyn D. Kedar*
Inspiring spiritual insight to guide you on your life journeys and teach you to live and thrive in two conflicting worlds: the rational/material and the spiritual.
6 x 9, 176 pp, Quality PB, ISBN 1-58023-202-7 **$16.99**

Also Available: **The Dance of the Dolphin** (Hardcover edition of *Our Dance with God*)
6 x 9, 176 pp, Hardcover, ISBN 1-58023-154-3 **$19.95**

The Empty Chair: Finding Hope and Joy—Timeless Wisdom from a Hasidic Master, Rebbe Nachman of Breslov *Adapted by the Breslov Research Institute*
4 x 6, 128 pp, 2-color text, Deluxe PB w/flaps, ISBN 1-879045-67-2 **$9.95**

The Gentle Weapon: Prayers for Everyday and Not-So-Everyday Moments—Timeless Wisdom from the Teachings of the Hasidic Master, Rebbe Nachman of Breslov
Adapted by Moshe Mykoff and S. C. Mizrahi, together with the Breslov Research Institute
4 x 6, 144 pp, 2-color text, Deluxe PB w/flaps, ISBN 1-58023-022-9 **$9.95**

God Whispers: Stories of the Soul, Lessons of the Heart *By Karyn D. Kedar*
6 x 9, 176 pp, Quality PB, ISBN 1-58023-088-1 **$15.95**

An Orphan in History: One Man's Triumphant Search for His Jewish Roots
By Paul Cowan. Afterword by Rachel Cowan. 6 x 9, 288 pp, Quality PB, ISBN 1-58023-135-7 **$16.95**

Restful Reflections: Nighttime Inspiration to Calm the Soul, Based on Jewish Wisdom
By Rabbi Kerry M. Olitzky & Rabbi Lori Forman 4½ x 6½, 448 pp, Quality PB, ISBN 1-58023-091-1 **$15.95**

Sacred Intentions: Daily Inspiration to Strengthen the Spirit, Based on Jewish Wisdom
By Rabbi Kerry M. Olitzky and Rabbi Lori Forman 4½ x 6½, 448 pp, Quality PB, ISBN 1-58023-061-X **$15.95**

Kabbalah/Mysticism/Enneagram

Awakening to Kabbalah: The Guiding Light of Spiritual Fulfillment
By Rav Michael Laitman, PhD
A distinctive, personal and awe-filled introduction to this ancient wisdom tradition.
6 x 9, 192 pp, Hardcover, ISBN 1-58023-264-7 **$21.99**

Seek My Face: A Jewish Mystical Theology
By Dr. Arthur Green
This classic work of contemporary Jewish theology, revised and updated, is a profound, deeply personal statement of the lasting truths of Jewish mysticism and the basic faith claims of Judaism. 6 x 9, 304 pp, Quality PB, ISBN 1-58023-130-6 **$19.95**

Zohar: Annotated & Explained
Translation and annotation by Dr. Daniel C. Matt. Foreword by Andrew Harvey
Offers insightful yet unobtrusive commentary to the masterpiece of Jewish mysticism. 5½ x 8½, 160 pp, Quality PB, ISBN 1-893361-51-9 **$15.99** *(A SkyLight Paths book)*

Cast in God's Image: Discover Your Personality Type Using the Enneagram and Kabbalah
By Rabbi Howard A. Addison
7 x 9, 176 pp, Quality PB, Layflat binding, 20+ journaling exercises, ISBN 1-58023-124-1 **$16.95**

Ehyeh: A Kabbalah for Tomorrow *By Dr. Arthur Green*
6 x 9, 224 pp, Quality PB, ISBN 1-58023-213-2 **$16.99;** Hardcover, ISBN 1-58023-125-X **$21.95**

The Enneagram and Kabbalah, 2nd Edition: Reading Your Soul
By Rabbi Howard A. Addison 6 x 9, 192 pp, Quality PB, ISBN 1-58023-229-9 **$16.99**

Finding Joy: A Practical Spiritual Guide to Happiness *By Dannel I. Schwartz with Mark Hass*
6 x 9, 192 pp, Quality PB, ISBN 1-58023-009-1 **$14.95**

The Gift of Kabbalah: Discovering the Secrets of Heaven, Renewing Your Life on Earth
By Tamar Frankiel, Ph.D.
6 x 9, 256 pp, Quality PB, ISBN 1-58023-141-1 **$16.95;** Hardcover, ISBN 1-58023-108-X **$21.95**

The Way Into Jewish Mystical Tradition *By Lawrence Kushner*
6 x 9, 224 pp, Quality PB, ISBN 1-58023-200-0 **$18.99;** Hardcover, ISBN 1-58023-029-6 **$21.95**

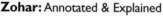

Spirituality/Lawrence Kushner

Filling Words with Light: Hasidic and Mystical Reflections on Jewish Prayer
By Lawrence Kushner and Nehemia Polen
Reflects on the joy, gratitude, mystery and awe embedded in traditional prayers and
blessings, and shows how you can imbue these familiar sacred words with your own
sense of holiness. 5½ x 8½, 176 pp, Hardcover, ISBN 1-58023-216-7 **$21.99**

The Book of Letters: A Mystical Hebrew Alphabet
Popular Hardcover Edition, 6 x 9, 80 pp, 2-color text, ISBN 1-879045-00-1 **$24.95**
Collector's Limited Edition, 9 x 12, 80 pp, gold foil embossed pages, w/limited edition silkscreened
print, ISBN 1-879045-04-4 **$349.00**

The Book of Miracles: A Young Person's Guide to Jewish Spiritual Awareness
6 x 9, 96 pp, 2-color illus., Hardcover, ISBN 1-879045-78-8 **$16.95** *For ages 9–13*

The Book of Words: Talking Spiritual Life, Living Spiritual Talk
6 x 9, 160 pp, Quality PB, ISBN 1-58023-020-2 **$16.95**

Eyes Remade for Wonder: A Lawrence Kushner Reader *Introduction by Thomas Moore*
6 x 9, 240 pp, Quality PB, ISBN 1-58023-042-3 **$18.95**; Hardcover, ISBN 1-58023-014-8 **$23.95**

God Was in This Place & I, i Did Not Know
Finding Self, Spirituality and Ultimate Meaning 6 x 9, 192 pp, Quality PB, ISBN 1-879045-33-8 **$16.95**

Honey from the Rock: An Introduction to Jewish Mysticism
6 x 9, 176 pp, Quality PB, ISBN 1-58023-073-3 **$16.95**

Invisible Lines of Connection: Sacred Stories of the Ordinary
5½ x 8½, 160 pp, Quality PB, ISBN 1-879045-98-2 **$15.95**

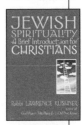

Jewish Spirituality—A Brief Introduction for Christians
5½ x 8½, 112 pp, Quality PB Original, ISBN 1-58023-150-0 **$12.95**

The River of Light: Jewish Mystical Awareness 6 x 9, 192 pp, Quality PB, ISBN 1-58023-096-2 **$16.95**

The Way Into Jewish Mystical Tradition
6 x 9, 224 pp, Quality PB, ISBN 1-58023-200-0 **$18.99**; Hardcover, ISBN 1-58023-029-6 **$21.95**

Spirituality/Prayer

Pray Tell: A Hadassah Guide to Jewish Prayer
*By Rabbi Jules Harlow, with contributions from Tamara Cohen, Rochelle Furstenberg, Rabbi Daniel
Gordis, Leora Tanenbaum, and many others*
Enriched with insight and wisdom from a broad variety of viewpoints.
8½ x 11, 400 pp, Quality PB, ISBN 1-58023-163-2 **$29.95**

My People's Prayer Book Series
Traditional Prayers, Modern Commentaries *Edited by Rabbi Lawrence A. Hoffman*
Provides diverse and exciting commentary to the traditional liturgy, helping modern
men and women find new wisdom in Jewish prayer, and bring liturgy into their lives.
Each book includes Hebrew text, modern translation, and commentaries from all
perspectives of the Jewish world.
Vol. 1—The *Sh'ma* and Its Blessings
7 x 10, 168 pp, Hardcover, ISBN 1-879045-79-6 **$24.99**
Vol. 2—The *Amidah*
7 x 10, 240 pp, Hardcover, ISBN 1-879045-80-X **$24.95**
Vol. 3—*P'sukei D'zimrah* (Morning Psalms)
7 x 10, 240 pp, Hardcover, ISBN 1-879045-81-8 **$24.95**
Vol. 4—*Seder K'riat Hatorah* (The Torah Service)
7 x 10, 264 pp, Hardcover, ISBN 1-879045-82-6 **$23.95**
Vol. 5—*Birkhot Hashachar* (Morning Blessings)
7 x 10, 240 pp, Hardcover, ISBN 1-879045-83-4 **$24.95**
Vol. 6—*Tachanun* and Concluding Prayers
7 x 10, 240 pp, Hardcover, ISBN 1-879045-84-2 **$24.95**
Vol. 7—Shabbat at Home
7 x 10, 240 pp, Hardcover, ISBN 1-879045-85-0 **$24.95**
Vol. 8—*Kabbalat Shabbat* (Welcoming Shabbat in the Synagogue)
7 x 10, 240 pp, Hardcover, ISBN 1-879045-121-7 **$24.99**
Vol. 9—Welcoming the Night: *Minchah* and *Ma'ariv* (Afternoon and
Evening Prayer) 7 x 10, 272 pp, Hardcover, ISBN 1-58023-262-0 **$24.99**

JEWISH LIGHTS BOOKS ARE AVAILABLE FROM BETTER BOOKSTORES. TRY YOUR BOOKSTORE FIRST.

About Jewish Lights

People of all faiths and backgrounds yearn for books that attract, engage, educate, and spiritually inspire.

Our principal goal is to stimulate thought and help all people learn about who the Jewish People are, where they come from, and what the future can be made to hold. While people of our diverse Jewish heritage are the primary audience, our books speak to people in the Christian world as well and will broaden their understanding of Judaism and the roots of their own faith.

We bring to you authors who are at the forefront of spiritual thought and experience. While each has something different to say, they all say it in a voice that you can hear.

Our books are designed to welcome you and then to engage, stimulate, and inspire. We judge our success not only by whether or not our books are beautiful and commercially successful, but by whether or not they make a difference in your life.

For your information and convenience, at the back of this book we have provided a list of other Jewish Lights books you might find interesting and useful. They cover all the categories of your life:

Bar/Bat Mitzvah	Life Cycle
Bible Study / Midrash	Meditation
Children's Books	Parenting
Congregation Resources	Prayer
Current Events / History	Ritual / Sacred Practice
Ecology	Spirituality
Fiction: Mystery, Science Fiction	Theology / Philosophy
Grief / Healing	Travel
Holidays / Holy Days	Twelve Steps
Inspiration	Women's Interest
Kabbalah / Mysticism / Enneagram	

Stuart M. Matlins, Publisher

Or phone, fax, mail or e-mail to: **JEWISH LIGHTS Publishing**
Sunset Farm Offices, Route 4 • P.O. Box 237 • Woodstock, Vermont 05091
Tel: (802) 457-4000 • Fax: (802) 457-4004 • www.jewishlights.com
Credit card orders: **(800) 962-4544** (8:30AM–5:30PM ET Monday–Friday)
Generous discounts on quantity orders. SATISFACTION GUARANTEED. Prices subject to change.

For more information about each book, visit our website at www.jewishlights.com